Bering Sea

NORTH ASIA

CENTRAL ASIA

⭐ Japan p46

⭐ Delhi p122

NORTH
PACIFIC
OCEAN

⭐ Chiang Mai
p130

Arabian
Sea

SOUTHEAST
ASIA

Bay of
Bengal

Equator

⭐
Gili Islands p88

The Marquesas Islands p60 ⭐

INDIAN
OCEAN

⭐ Vanuatu p30

⭐ Great Barrier Reef
p76

AUSTRALASIA
& OCEANIA

⭐ Newcastle
p126

Tasman
Sea

⭐ Wellington
p106

SOUTHERN
OCEAN

LONELY PLANET'S

BEST IN TRAVEL
2011

THE BEST TRENDS, DESTINATIONS, JOURNEYS & EXPERIENCES FOR THE UPCOMING YEAR

MELBOURNE ✪ OAKLAND ✪ LONDON

CONTENTS

FOREWORD

YOUR TRAVELLING YEAR STARTS HERE, WITH *BEST IN TRAVEL 2011*. THIS BOOK IS FULL OF FRESH IDEAS FOR WHERE TO GO AND WHAT TO SEE TO GIVE YOU THE INSPIRATION TO GET OUT AND EXPLORE THIS YEAR, NEAR OR FAR. DO THIS NOW: GET THAT DIARY OUT AND BLOCK OUT SOME TIME OFF BEFORE IT'S GONE – YOU'RE GOING TO NEED IT.

This book started with hundreds of ideas from everyone at Lonely Planet, including our extended family of travellers, bloggers and tweeters. These ideas were whittled down by a panel of in-house travel experts, including Lonely Planet co-founder Tony Wheeler, based on scores for topicality, excitement, value for money and that special X-factor. As a result of this voting system, 2011 marks the first time our top 10 countries, regions and cities are ranked in order. We've put them out there – now we're looking forward to the debates that come next.

Where to first? Top scoring destinations to visit this year are Europe's last frontier, Albania (p10); Egypt's fast-changing Sinai Peninsula (p52) and endlessly exciting New York City (p94). The trend for rediscovering classics sees Italy (p34), Cappadocia in Turkey (p64) and the West Coast of the USA (p80) ranked highly by our experts. There are plenty of surprises too, from little-known countries like Cape Verde and Vanuatu to Iceland's wild Westfjords peninsula, Tangier in Morocco, and – yes really – Newcastle in Australia.

2011's top travel lists make for revealing reading. Most of us can only dream of the private tropical island and custom-built submarine favoured by the super-luxe brigade (p144), but everyone likes a good deal – start planning with this year's list of best-value destinations on p136. The world doesn't stand still, so while suggesting 10 places to head to for communist nostalgia (p152) we also highlight 10 countries that didn't even exist when the Berlin Wall fell (p156). Suggestions for eating and learning to cook, dancing and shopping reflect enduring passions. There are, as ever, some interesting new niches: vampire-spotting locales (p196), anyone?

Whether 2011 takes you from the idyllic Marquesas to windswept Chilean Patagonia, diving Indonesia's Gili Islands or strolling the medieval lanes of Ghent in Belgium, this year promises to be a wonderful one for globe-trotters. This book offers a kick-start to your best adventures yet.

Tom Hall, Lonely Planet Travel Editor

010
ALBANIA

014
BRAZIL

018
CAPE VERDE

022
PANAMA

026
BULGARIA

LONELY PLANET'S
TOP 10 COUNTRIES

030
VANUATU

034
ITALY

038
TANZANIA

042
SYRIA

046
JAPAN

○ ALBANIA

'The jig is almost up – Albania won't be off the beaten track for much longer.'

By Marika McAdam

`01`

ALBANIA

- ✪ **POPULATION** 3.6 MILLION
- ✪ **FOREIGN VISITORS PER YEAR** AROUND 6 MILLION
- ✪ **CAPITAL** TIRANA
- ✪ **LANGUAGE** ALBANIAN
- ✪ **MAJOR INDUSTRIES** MAJOR EXPORTS ARE CHROMIUM AND CHROME PRODUCTS
- ✪ **UNIT OF CURRENCY** LEKË
- ✪ **COST INDEX** TIRANA BEER 150 LEKË (US$1.50), MIDRANGE HOTEL DOUBLE 8000 LEKË (US$80), SHORT TAXI RIDE 300 LEKË (US$3), INTERNET ACCESS PER HOUR 100 LEKË (US$1), BOTTLE OF ALBANIAN WINE 600 LEKË (US$6), FERRY TO CORFU, GREECE 2000 LEKË (US$20)

SIME/PAVAN ALDO » 4CORNERS

YOU COULDN'T MAKE THIS STUFF UP

Picture, if you will, a place where rulers have names like King Zog, Enver Hoxha and Bamir Topi. Now make it the headquarters of the mystical Bektashi Order. Set the scene with coastal cliffs, snow-capped mountains and jungle-wrapped ruins. Cast some female 'sworn virgins' to fill the roles of men who have been lost in ancient blood feuds. Let the spoken dialects be known as Tosk and Gheg. Make it that daily life is governed by a code of conduct with 1262 instructions including 38 on hospitality towards guests.

It may seem like you've just conjured a medieval fantasy novel rather than an up-and-coming travel destination, but this is Albania in all its epic, eclectic glory.

THE LAST OF THE LAST FRONTIERS

Not so long ago, when the Balkans were considered an 'only for the brave' travel destination, only the bravest of the brave trickled into Albania. Since backpackers started coming to elusive Albania in the 1990s, tales have been told in 'keep it to yourself' whispers of azure beaches, confrontingly good cuisine, heritage sites, nightlife, affordable adventures and the possibility of old-style unplanned journeys complete with open-armed locals for whom travellers are still a novelty. Sick to death of being dismissed with blinged-up crime-boss clichés, Albania has announced 'A New Mediterranean Love' via its tourist board. The jig is almost up – Albania won't be off the beaten track for much longer.

DEFINING EXPERIENCE

If you are a journey-over-destination kind of traveller, take the road (and a sick bag) from Korça to Gjirokastra. The road climbs along the Greek border to the highlands, slices through pine forests along the edge of the Gramoz mountains before crossing the Barmash Pass (1759m) and descending dramatically into the narrow valley of the Vjosa River and up the Drinos valley. Recover down south on the beach at Dhërmi or take the ferry from Saranda across the Ionian sea to the Greek Islands, just because you can.

TONY WHEELER » LPI

FINDING SOME FUN IN ALBANIA WON'T BE AN UPHILL BATTLE – TIRANA'S PYRAMID (FORMERLY THE ENVER HOXHA MUSEUM)

PAVING THE WAY TO THE WEST

Traversable roads and terrain cleared of the scourge of landmines are the new black in this part of the world. Albania is working towards the goal of being a landmine-free nation in 2011, and various improvements to infrastructure mean that the so-called 'roads' in some parts of the country will hopefully soon cast off their inverted commas.

TIRANA TUNES

✪ The annual Tirana International Film Festival is a multiday, multigenre film bonanza attracting flickerati from around the world. The ninth festival will be held at the end of 2011.

✪ Since the turn of the millennium, the Tirana Jazz Festival, held in June or July every year, has made for smooth and sweaty summers in the Albanian capital.

WHAT'S HOT... / WHAT'S NOT...

Many locals will probably admit to having lost their virginity in a concrete bunker left over from last century's Hoxha era. However, as there are more people who claim to have urinated in these ubiquitous cubicles than there are people who say they have bonked in one of these many bunkers, think twice before you rush to join the Concrete Club.

ALL THE RAGE OR ALL ENRAGED?

The 2011 census is set to be a snapshot – albeit a blurred one – of a country that never sits still. Will it cast light on the shadows or stir up divisions and derision? The answer may impact Albania's aspiration for candidature in the EU in this same year.

RANDOM FACTS

✪ Two Nobel Prize winners of ethnic Albanian descent took different paths to greatness. India's Mother Teresa may have miraculously cured a tumour, while another kind of miracle was performed by America's Professor Ferid Murad, the inventor of Viagra.

✪ Albania is one of the few countries in Europe to have had more Jews after WWII than before.

✪ The glass pyramid, which was once a museum to iron-fisted Hoxha, was designed by the Comrade's own daughter and son-in-law.

MOST BIZARRE SIGHT

✪ Artificially terraced hills – the product of Hoxha's kooky agricultural brainwave to level hills into fields.

'Famous for samba, football and cinematic scenery, Brazil has always been known for celebration…'

By Regis St Louis

02

BRAZIL

- ✪ **POPULATION** 200 MILLION
- ✪ **FOREIGN VISITORS PER YEAR** 5.1 MILLION
- ✪ **CAPITAL** BRASÍLIA
- ✪ **LANGUAGE** PORTUGUESE
- ✪ **MAJOR INDUSTRIES** AGRICULTURE, MINING, TEXTILES
- ✪ **UNIT OF CURRENCY** BRAZILIAN REAL (R$)
- ✪ **COST INDEX** COCONUT WATER ON THE BEACH/DRAFT OF BRAHMA BEER R$3/4 (US$1.70/2.25), HOTEL DOUBLE/DORM ROOM IN IPANEMA FROM R$240/50 (US$134/28), SAMBA CLUB ENTRANCE R$15–30 (US$8–17), INTERNET ACCESS PER HOUR R$6 (US$3.40)

VIVIANE PONTI » LPI

THE FUTURE IS NOW

Brazil can finally lay to rest that old jibe that it is 'the country of the future and always will be.' The country of perpetual promise has made astounding gains over the past few years, dramatically curbing poverty while growing its middle class to become the majority for the first time in the nation's history. The world's ninth-largest economy emerged from the global financial crisis faster and healthier than most, all the while investing in public infrastructure and bringing peace to some of the country's most violent *favelas* (shanty towns). Many Brazilians attribute the success to the charismatic Luiz Inácio Lula da Silva, the shoeshine-boy-turned-president, who ended his second term with record-high approval ratings (more than 70%).

READY FOR TAKE-OFF

Famous for samba, football and cinematic scenery, Brazil has always been known for celebration (Carnaval being the most obvious manifestation of this national *joie de vivre*). Yet, Brazil rings in 2011 with even more cause for jubilation. Winning the bids to host both the 2014 FIFA World Cup and the 2016 Summer Olympics in Rio de Janeiro, Brazil is undertaking a flurry of new projects, with billions of dollars earmarked for infrastructure (there's even discussion of building a high-speed rail line between Rio and São Paulo). Despite the strong Brazilian real, travellers should benefit from the addition of thousands of new hotel rooms, while increased competition from low-cost airline carriers (including Azul, established by the Brazilian-born founder of JetBlue) should make travel across this vast country more affordable.

DEFINING EXPERIENCE

Stroll Rio's Copacabana beach in the early morning, followed by an *açaí* drink (made from the touted Amazonian berry) at the nearest juice bar. Afterwards, join the beauty crowd on Ipanema beach, followed by a bang-up all-you-can-eat feast at a *churrascaria* (barbecue-meat restaurant). Catch the sunset (coconut water in hand) from Arpoador, then end the night in Lapa, where dozens of samba clubs keep the music going until dawn.

FESTIVALS & EVENTS

✪ Don a costume and dance through the streets, perhaps racking up a few sins along the way, in the pre-Lenten revelry of Carnaval (4–8 March). Celebrations are at their liveliest in Rio, Salvador and Recife.

✪ In São Luís, locals sing, dance and sometimes dress up as oxen at the colourful folkloric festival Bumba Meu Boi (13–30 June).

✪ Forget chilly Times Square, lovely Copacabana beach is the place to ring in the new year during Reveillon (31 December). Wear white to bring good luck in 2012.

LIFE-CHANGING EXPERIENCES

✪ Paddling a dugout canoe along Amazonian *igarapés* (tiny rivers) in search of macaws, monkeys, river dolphins and, gulp, anacondas.

✪ Soaring over the forest-covered mountains and stunning beaches of Rio on a hang-gliding flight off Pedra Bonita.

✪ Hearing the thunderous roar of Iguaçu on a boat ride near (but not too close) to the edge of the awe-inspiring waterfalls.

HOT TOPICS OF THE DAY

Poverty! Social inequality! And for once the news isn't all bad. Brazil continues to make enormous strides toward narrowing the gap between haves and have-nots. Over the last decade Brazil has led Latin America in absolute poverty reduction with more than 10 million people leaving slum conditions.

RANDOM FACTS

✪ Home to the Amazon rainforest, Brazil has more known plant and animal species than any other country on earth, including 1780 bird species, 80 primate species and five of the world's seven species of sea turtles.

✪ Brazil has 17 Unesco World Heritage Sites, including the Serra da Capivara National Park, with some of the oldest cave paintings in the Americas.

✪ São Paulo has the world's largest Japanese community outside of Japan.

MOST BIZARRE SIGHT

Mucky, brown, cayman-filled rivers aren't exactly a big draw for surfers – unless you're talking about the National Pororoca Surfing Championship, held on the Rio Guamá near the mouth of the Amazon. The powerful wave here appears just a few times a year, created by an unusual tidal bore around the spring equinox. That's when extreme surfers paddle onto the debris-filled river to ride churning swells up to 4m high, travelling speeds of 30km/h and sometimes getting a long sweet journey. The record is a 12.5km ride that lasted 37 minutes.

RICARDO GOMES » LPI

IT'S A VOLLEYBALL ECLIPSE ON IPANEMA BEACH, RIO DE JANEIRO

'Cape Verdeans might have known about the wider world forever, but it seems that the wider world is only just opening its eyes to Cape Verde.'

NORTH AMERICA

ASIA

CAPE VERDE ✪

AFRICA

SOUTH AMERICA

AUSTRALIA

By Stuart Butler

`03`

CAPE VERDE

✪ **POPULATION** 429,474

✪ **FOREIGN VISITORS PER YEAR** 285,000

✪ **CAPITAL** PRAIA

✪ **LANGUAGES** CRIOULO, PORTUGUESE

✪ **MAJOR INDUSTRIES** TOURISM, FISHING

✪ **UNIT OF CURRENCY** CAPE VERDE ESCUDO (CVE)

✪ **COST INDEX** BUDGET/MIDRANGE HOTEL DOUBLE CVE2000/4000 (US$27/54), SHORT TAXI RIDE CVE150 (US$2), INTERNET ACCESS PER HOUR CVE100 (US$1.35), SAL–SANTIAGO FLIGHT CVE6000 (US$80), WINDSURF RENTAL CVE4000 (US$55)

ALEX3 » DREAMSTIME

BLINK AND YOU'LL MISS THEM

Cape Verdeans might have known about the wider world forever, but it seems that the wider world is only just opening its eyes to Cape Verde. On the surface this is hardly a surprise; the country appears to be nothing but a blink-and-you'll-miss-it dot of dust floating off the coast of Africa, but the islands have recently started catching sideways glances from European winter-sun tourists. This growing international interest is bringing enormous changes to an archipelago that looks and feels as if it were born from a Caribbean mother and an African father.

PSF » IMAGEBROKER

THE NEXT BIG THING

But what is it that these tourists come for and why is now the time to go? When someone first mentioned trying to attract foreign visitors to their 'dot of dust' most Cape Verdeans must have laughingly thought 'What can we offer a tourist here?'. The answer turned out to be quite a lot. Soaring mountains terraced in greens, a volcano with its head in the clouds, world-class watersports and sizzling, saucy festivals – but it was the sun that clinched the deal. With almost more days of sunshine than there are days in the year and with soft sandy beaches to boot, someone only had to say the words 'winter sun' and the islands were being marketed as the 'New Canary Islands'. And that's why the time to go is now. Figures show that tourism arrivals are increasing by a staggering 22% a year and the government hopes to attract a million visitors a year by 2015. As we all know, a million people can't be wrong – just make sure you get there before them!

DEFINING EXPERIENCE

Soak up the atmosphere as a procession of seductive hip-swaying dancing girls with pompoms and feather boas prances past during Mardi Gras, then hop from bar to bar around the cultural capital Mindelo, feast on the country's famous fresh lobsters, and finally unwind on the beaches at Santa Maria, a windsurfer's mecca.

RECENT FAD

More and more visitors have been discarding the beachside flip-flops and donning hiking boots in order to hit the trails of the dizzyingly vertical island of Santo Antão. Try scrambling up the cinder cone of Mt Fogo, hiking the back lanes of Santiago or even breaking new ground in remote and rugged Brava.

FESTIVALS & EVENTS

✪ Taking the best African beats and mixing it up with a healthy dose of Latin style and Brazilian sex appeal, Mindelo's Mardi Gras celebration, which takes place 5–8 March 2011, is one sultry, raunchy party you'll never forget.

✪ Cape Verdeans live and breathe music. The first of the major music festivals that rock the islands year round is the Festival de Musica Gambõa (Gambõa Music Festival), held on the beach in Praia for three days from 19 May.

✪ Come August and the musical frenzy in Cape Verde reaches a peak with the huge Festival de Musica Baía das Gatas (Baía das Gatas Music Festival), an event that sees big-name stars from Cape Verde and beyond rocking out on the sands of Baía das Gatas beach.

LIFE-CHANGING EXPERIENCES

✪ Splashing about with the turtles of Boa Vista on a turtle-watching tour.

✪ Throwing down a forward loop or two at the end of a windsurfing course or racing the tube on a surfboard at Punta Preta.

✪ Playing at Lawrence of Arabia on a desert safari on any of the eastern isles.

✪ Putting your best foot forward on any of the innumerable hiking trails weaving across the western isles.

✪ Strumming a guitar and singing like the lark of Cape Verde, Cesária Évora.

RANDOM FACTS

✪ The name Cape Verde (Green Headland) actually refers to a place in Senegal.

✪ Around 80 endemic species of plant call the islands home.

✪ The UN rates the standard of living in Cape Verde as the highest in West Africa.

✪ Founded in 1462, Cidade Velha is the oldest European town in the tropics.

MOST BIZARRE SIGHT

OK, so it's more of a most bizarre night than a bizarre sight, but on the island of Fogo you can relish the excitement of sleeping in a hotel built inside the crater of a live and brooding volcano – sweet dreams!

'...Panama occupies a continental crossroads where the 21st century meets the dawn of the ages.'

EUROPE

NORTH AMERICA

ASIA

◇ PANAMA

AFRICA

SOUTH AMERICA

AUSTRALIA

By Carolyn McCarthy

PANAMA

- ✪ **POPULATION** 3.4 MILLION
- ✪ **FOREIGN VISITORS PER YEAR** 1.3 MILLION
- ✪ **CAPITAL** PANAMA CITY
- ✪ **LANGUAGES** SPANISH, ENGLISH, INDIGENOUS LANGUAGES
- ✪ **MAJOR INDUSTRY** SERVICES, PRIMARILY PANAMA CANAL OPERATIONS AND BANKING
- ✪ **UNIT OF CURRENCY** US DOLLAR (US$)
- ✪ **COST INDEX** BOTTLE OF BALBOA BEER US$1, DORM BED IN BOCAS DEL TORO US$7, CEVICHE FOR TWO US$4, OPEN-WATER SCUBA COURSE US$275

BLING & BIODIVERSITY

The belly button of the Americas, Panama has rhythms that hip-hop between modern and primitive, such as the line of skyscrapers and container ships set against clear seas and dense, dark rainforest not so far away. For many, the culture of commerce has defined this tiny tropical nation, best known as the world's most famous shortcut. Yet its treasures – from millennial indigenous cultures to a biodiversity that astounds – run far deeper. Panama was always there, but who *knew?* On the world map and in the ether of sentiment, Panama occupies a continental crossroads where the 21st century meets the dawn of the ages.

ERIC WHEATER » LPI

THE EMBERÁ AND WOUNAAN PEOPLE USE PURPLE TAGUA JUICE ON THEIR BODIES FOR HEALTH REASONS

BACK TO ESSENTIALS

For Panama, the world economic crisis offered a perfect excuse to hit the reset button. After an unchecked growth spurt created a clutter of casinos, gated communities and glass towers in the name of Trump, the investment slump has forced a return to basics. For travellers, there's a return to the authentic – local heartland festivals, jungle treks and lodgings in sand-floor huts in the independent Comarca de Kuna Yala. With plenty of the country still pristine, true adventure is only a boat or bus fare away.

In 2011 Panama City gets greener, with the anticipated unveiling of the BíoMuseo, an innovative Frank Gehry–designed space celebrating ecological diversity. Panama City's new Cinta Costera (Coastal Belt) creates a green stripe of waterfront paths that finishes in Casco Viejo, a stunning historic neighbourhood remade after decades of neglect. Like elsewhere, climate change and habitat destruction are taking their toll here. Panama's inch-long golden frogs, victims of a worldwide epidemic, are fast disappearing. But the Darién Gap, considered one of the world's wildest places, still remains roadless. Countless Panamanian islands persist without name or a sole inhabitant.

Costa Rica eat your heart out.

DEFINING EXPERIENCE

Buzzing up jungle rivers in a dugout canoe to Emberá-Wounaan communities where online defines a phone booth encircled by thatched huts and chatting means negotiating the offer to be painted chin to elbow in purple tagua juice.

FESTIVALS & EVENTS

✪ In mid-January, the Panama Jazz Festival draws international artists to jam in Casco Viejo's open-air plaza; the main event is free for spectators.

ALFREDO MAIQUEZ » LPI

NATURE AT ITS BRILLIANT BEST – THE COLOUR-CHANGING STRAWBERRY POISON FROG, BOCAS DEL TORO

✪ Portobelo's biannual Festival de Diablos y Congos celebrates rebellion and liberty in March. Re-enacting history, locals assume the role of escaped slaves and take 'captives' for token ransoms.

✪ Feria de la Mejorana is Panama's largest folkloric festival, with dancing and decorated ox-carts parading rum-soaked streets; it's held every September on the tradition-rich Azuero Peninsula.

LIFE-CHANGING EXPERIENCES

✪ Searching for harpy eagles in the ultraremote Parque Nacional Darién.

✪ Scaling Barú Volcano for a panorama that spans the Atlantic and Pacific oceans.

✪ Diving with the world's largest fish, a school-bus-sized whale shark, in Parque Nacional Coiba.

✪ Watching over nesting hawksbill turtles on the Azuero Peninsula.

✪ Sailing the stunning San Blás Archipelago, home to virgin islets and vibrant Kuna communities.

WHAT'S HOT...

Boquete's award-winning gesha coffee beans, sold for more than US$100 per pound; the new TransPanama Trail trekking route; revitalised Casco Viejo.

WHAT'S NOT...

Gated communities geared at foreign retirees.

HOT TOPIC OF THE DAY

An ambitious US$5 billion project is expanding the Panama Canal. This massive makeover – slated for completion in 2014 – should bring more canal traffic including larger vessels for a much-needed boost to the economy.

RANDOM FACTS

✪ Panama has 21 times more plant species than Brazil per sq km.

✪ Panama has 950 avian species, the largest number in Central America.

✪ The Panama Canal's toll revenue nears US$4 million.

✪ 22,000 workers died trying to construct the original canal.

MOST BIZARRE SIGHT

A lost world of pristine ecosystems and unique fauna, Parque Nacional Coiba has remained intact for bizarre reasons. The former home of a notorious penal colony, Coiba Island had an infallible security system: nature. Today visitors can snorkel with turtles, dive with whale sharks and peruse jungle spotted with crumbling prison cells overtaken by vines.

EUROPE

○ BULGARIA

NORTH
AMERICA

AFRICA

ASIA

SOUTH
AMERICA

AUSTRALIA

'…Bulgaria has always had its moments – in its biggest cities, on its snow-capped peaks and great-value ski fields…'

By Robert Reid

05

BULGARIA

- ○ **POPULATION** 7.2 MILLION
- ○ **FOREIGN VISITORS PER YEAR** 7 MILLION
- ○ **CAPITAL** SOFIA
- ○ **LANGUAGE** BULGARIAN
- ○ **MAJOR INDUSTRIES** ELECTRICITY, GAS
- ○ **UNIT OF CURRENCY** LEVA (LV)
- ○ **COST INDEX** CUP OF COFFEE 0.80 LV (US$0.55), HOTEL DOUBLE/DORM FROM 50/20 LV (US$35/14), SHORT TAXI RIDE FROM 5 LV (US$3.50), INTERNET ACCESS PER HOUR 1 LV (US$0.70)

SIME/ MORANDI BRUNO » 4CORNERS

COMING-OUT PARTY

For those who looked, Bulgaria has always had its moments – in its biggest cities, on its snow-capped peaks and great-value ski fields, on its golden-sand beaches and in ancient Black Sea port towns. Let's not forget its enduring traditions such as the locals' tendency to shake their heads 'yes' and nod them 'no.'

Yet, over the years, with history's contribution, Bulgaria has got lost amid its more famous neighbours. From the south, the Ottoman soldiers of present-day Turkey ran Bulgaria for 500 years. Legendary toga-clad Greeks to the south mocked Bulgaria's strong wines (before adopting the same). More recently, the Romanians claimed the share of fame via distinguishing Latin bloodlines and Transylvania's mystic, fangy appeal. Bulgaria sometimes feels like the odd guy out in this corner of Europe.

But things are changing. Now proudly part of the 21st-century EU, Bulgaria has enjoyed more attention – and self confidence. Its ski slopes are de facto destinations for Europeans looking for cheaper alternatives, empty patches of lovely Black Sea beaches can *still* be found, and its quietly brilliant wine industry is flourishing. Even remote Belogradchik's unreal fortress made it on a short list for the 2011 New Wonders of the World.

Whatever happens, Bulgarians will take it in their stride. As one local song goes, 'We win, we lose…either way we get drunk, we're Bulgarians!' That oughta be on a T-shirt.

SOMEWHERE IN BULGARIA THERE'S A FIELD OF COWS WITHOUT THEIR BELLS – DURING THE KUKERI FESTIVAL AT LEAST

JTB PHOTO » PHOTOLIBRARY

DEFINING EXPERIENCE

Eat a hot *banitsa* (cheese-filled pastry) for breakfast while studying the Cyrillic alphabet (that's right: it's a Bulgarian creation, not a Russian one), then pop into a folksy 19th-century revival-era *kâshta* (traditional home; Plovdiv's Old Town or Koprivshtitsa have loads of them). Finish the day with great Bulgarian wines (like the hangover-free reds in Melnik) – it's only fitting here in the birthplace of Dionysus, the Greek god of wine.

FESTIVALS & EVENTS

✪ Held on the Sunday before Lent (March in 2011), the *kukeri* festival looks like a Chewbacca pyjama party, with revellers in hairy costumes warding off evil spirits. Best seen in the Rodopi village of Shiroka Lûka.

✪ As part of *martenitsa* in March, Bulgarians exchange red-and-white figures that they wear until they see a stork, after which they tie the figures to a tree. Good thing there's not a shortage of storks about.

✪ The coastal town of Kavarna transforms into the 'Heavy Metal Capital of the World' on the last weekend in June, when the local rock-fest attracts metal bands and long-haired enthusiasts. Year round you can see metal-god murals on central housing blocks. Long live Uriah Heep!

LIFE-CHANGING EXPERIENCES

✪ Lugging your beach towel over Black Sea cliffs to remote golden-sand beaches (sometimes clothing optional) at Sinemorets near the Turkish border.

✪ Hiking in the central Stara Planina mountain range, passing the streamside Dryanovo Monastery and stumbling upon long-neglected Roman roads.

✪ Bar hopping with Sofia's university students in the surreal Studentski Grad, where Stalin-esque dorms have been transformed into late-night clubs, music venues and karaoke bars. As one student put it: 'It's hard to learn anything when you're always hung over.'

RANDOM FACTS

Much of the central valley around Kazanlâk is littered with Thracian *mogila* (burial mounds), and since the fall of communism, there's been something of a race between archaeologists and grave robbers to find them first. One of the most impressive monuments is the recently opened Kosmatka, site of the 5th-century tomb of Sevt III. The nearby Thracian town of Sevtopolis rests at the bottom of a dam-made lake, but there has been extravagant talk of emptying and walling the site to create a surreal tourist attraction reached by boat!

MOST BIZARRE SIGHT

A candidate for the New Seven Wonders of the World list (to be announced in 2011), Belogradchik in Bulgaria's 'pinkie' to the northwest looks like a setting too spooky for *The Lord of the Rings*, with a fort built by Romans then Ottomans straddling rock formations so lifelike they're named after people.

'For those in search of authentic experiences, Vanuatu is hard to beat. From mighty mountains and thunderous waterfalls to remote villages…'

○ VANUATU

By Jean-Bernard Carillet

06

VANUATU

○ **POPULATION** 215,000

○ **FOREIGN VISITORS PER YEAR** 83,000

○ **CAPITAL** PORT VILA

○ **LANGUAGES** BISLAMA, ENGLISH, FRENCH AND MORE THAN 105 LOCAL LANGUAGES

○ **MAJOR INDUSTRIES** AGRICULTURE, TOURISM

○ **UNIT OF CURRENCY** VATU (VT)

○ **COST INDEX** GLASS OF BEER 500VT (US$5), DOUBLE ROOM IN A TRADITIONAL GUESTHOUSE 4000VT (US$40), *KASTOM* VILLAGE TOUR 2000VT (US$20), A DIVE TO THE SS *PRESIDENT COOLIDGE* 6500VT (US$65)

PETER HENDRIE » LPI

LAVA & MAGMA

Scene: Mt Yasur, Tanna island, at dusk. Close up: a silhouette of people walking along a path, with golden fireworks in the background. Soundtrack: whooshing, roaring and, suddenly a gasp, a bang. The ground trembles and a fountain of fiery magma shoots up and spreads against the sky. Dante's *Inferno*? No, it's just routine in Vanuatu. Here the mountains murmur, yell, stink, smoke and shoot wild pyrotechnics high in the sky for fun. Furious Mt Yasur is one of the world's most accessible active volcanoes. Locals believe that it's the originator of the universe, and that it's where a person's spirit goes after death. On Gaua, sulphurous smoke belches so voluminously from Mt Garet that it tastes like you're sucking matches. On Paama, the perfect cone of Lopevi beckons and can be climbed, too; just pray she behaves while you walk across the ash plains.

BACK TO NATURE

For those in search of authentic experiences, Vanuatu is hard to beat. From mighty mountains and thunderous waterfalls to remote villages, from huge lagoons to tropical islets, there's so much on offer, far from the crowds. Don't expect ritzy resorts and Cancun-style nightlife; with a good choice of family-run guesthouses in traditional villages and a smattering of comfortable, romantic hideaways, it's tailor-made for ecotourists. With 83 islands, you're spoilt for choice. Vanuatu has recently seen an increased number of direct flights from Australia, New Zealand, New Caledonia, Fiji and the Solomon Islands – go now, before the secret's out.

WILL SALTER » LPI

THE FOURTH DIMENSION

More than any other of the South Pacific countries, Vanuatu emanates mystic vibes. Christianity, cargo cult (where believers act like Europeans so that wealth 'cargo' will come their way), *kastom* (the rules surrounding ancient ancestral legacies and customs) and even black magic are important, and all natural phenomena have a fourth dimension of spirituality and mystique. Traditions are strong and alive. On Malekula, you may still see old men with elongated heads. Why? Male babies' heads were wrapped tightly, so the soft skull bone was moulded high, in a shape that later made men look more distinguished.

DEFINING EXPERIENCE

On Tanna, get caught up in the tribal atmosphere during a village visit with the hypnotic banging of the *tamtams* and harmonic voices of the villagers; learn how *kava* (a mildly intoxicating drink) is prepared; and tuck into a delicious *laplap* (Vanuatu's national dish) before curling up in your bungalow built of all-natural jungle materials.

FESTIVALS & EVENTS

✪ One of the most powerful festivals in the South Pacific is Naghol (land-diving). On Pentecost island, every year from April to early June, men and boys hurtle from rickety structures with only two long, springy lianas (vines) to break their fall. Awesome!

✪ Vanuatu's most important annual event is Independence Day, on 30 July. It means celebrations everywhere, but Vila is the epicentre, with sporting events, a military parade, canoe races, string band competitions and *kastom* dancing.

LIFE-CHANGING EXPERIENCES

✪ Flipper-kicking into the SS *President Coolidge*, the world's largest accessible luxury liner and WWII wreck, off Espiritu Santo.

✪ Seeing master carvers at work and shopping for handicrafts on Ambrym.

✪ Hiking up to old cannibal sites and into spirit caves on Malekula.

✪ Snorkelling with a resident dugong on Epi.

✪ Taking a guided walk through misty cloudforest to a mystical world of colourful crater lakes on Ambae.

RANDOM FACTS

✪ Vanuatu claims the highest concentration of different languages per head of population of any country in the world.

✪ The people on Ambae island are known as intellectuals; most of the business directors and 80% of university students in Vila are from Ambae.

✪ Becoming a chief on Pentecost is expensive – an aspirant might kill more than 100 pigs.

✪ Vanuatu has nine active volcanoes – seven on land and two under the sea. Active fumaroles and thermal springs are often used for cooking food.

MOST BIZARRE SIGHT

On Ambae, Lake Manaro Lakua spreads blue-grey around the island's centre. It's the highest lake in the South Pacific. A few metres away, and 57m lower, the beautiful lime-green, hot Lake Vui sends vulcanologists into a frenzy whenever it starts to boil.

EUROPE
ITALY
NORTH AMERICA
ASIA
AFRICA
AMERICA

'The food is delicious, sunshine is plentiful, scenery and towns are sublime, and there is millennia-worth of art to look at.'

By Abigail Hole

07

ITALY

○ **POPULATION**: 58.1 MILLION

○ **FOREIGN VISITORS PER YEAR** 43 MILLION

○ **CAPITAL** ROME

○ **LANGUAGE** ITALIAN

○ **MAJOR INDUSTRIES** TOURISM, MANUFACTURING

○ **UNIT OF CURRENCY** EURO (€)

○ **COST INDEX** CAPPUCCINO €0.90 (US$1.20), HOTEL DOUBLE/DORM ROOM FOR A NIGHT €50–100/€10–20 (US$67–134/13–27), INTERNET ACCESS PER HOUR €3 (US$4), MARGHERITA PIZZA €3–4 (US$4–5)

BRENT WINEBRENNER » LPI

OH...THE BEAUTIFUL COUNTRY

Italy is a beguiling, beautiful, charismatic mess. The press might be largely owned by Prime Minister Silvio Berlusconi, stories of corruption, bribery and sex scandals might be everyday news, and the economy might be in the doldrums, but this is still one of the world's most magnificent places to be. The food is delicious, sunshine is plentiful, scenery and towns are sublime, and there is millennia-worth of art to look at. There are 44 Unesco World Heritage Sites here, more than in any other country.

JIGSAW NATION

That Italy is celebrating only 150 years as a country this year (it was unified in 1861) highlights how clearly it still feels like a collection of regions. Local people hail from their region; their nationality comes second. Each region has a pronounced character and qualities worthy of the small nations they once were, which makes it particularly rewarding to explore Italy bit by bit.

ITALIAN DISCOVERIES

With the euro maintaining its value and thus making travel here more expensive, now is the time to discover off-the-beaten-track (and thus usually better-value) regions that have been favourites with Italian holidaymakers for aeons: for example, Puglia and Calabria in the south, with their gleaming white beaches, towns perched atop dramatic sea cliffs and delicious, fresh-from-the-field gastronomy. Or you could discover the unsung beauty of Lazio, head to the volcanic-sanded coast of Basilicata, visit the elegiac Habsburg splendour of Trieste, or explore Sicily's outlying islands, such as remote Pantelleria and volcanic Stromboli.

DEFINING EXPERIENCE

Start with an early-morning dip in the powder-blue seas off a blinding-white Pugliese beach. Drive in a convertible along the rollercoaster Maratea coast, then negotiate the madness of Naples traffic and encounter the power of Pompeii. Down an espresso in Rome, and get lost in the capital's incredible splendours: ancient, medieval and baroque. Meander around Renaissance Florence and stay in a hilltop Tuscan villa. Dine in Bologna, capital of the state that brought us parmesan, parma ham and unparalleled *ragù* (meat sauce). Float through Venice and shop for killer threads in Milan.

RECENT FAD

Superfast trains: this year, Nuovo Trasporto Viaggiatori (NTV) is priming its new fleet of 25 French Automotrice à Grande Vitesse (AGV) trains to provide 300km/h services on the Turin–Milan–Naples–Salerno, Rome–Bologna–Venice and Rome–Naples–Bari routes.

WITOLD SKRYPCZAK » LPI

THERE'S A ROOM WITH A VIEW WAITING FOR YOU AT LAGO DI MISURINA IN THE DOLOMITI BELLUNESI NATIONAL PARK

FESTIVALS & EVENTS

✪ Throughout 2011, Turin – Italy's first capital – will celebrate the 150th anniversary of the Unification of Italy, with theatre, concerts and contemporary art exhibitions. Concerts and festivals during the year include the inauguration (17 March), with a recital of Verdi's *I Vespri Siciliani*.

✪ Carnival (this year beginning in late February) is celebrated all over Italy, most famously and fabulously in Venice, with seaside Viareggio in Tuscany coming a close second. But you'll find fancy dress, parties, confetti throwing and celebratory sweets all over the country.

✪ This year the Palio delle Quattro Antiche Repubbliche Marinare (Regatta of the Four Ancient Maritime Republics) will take place in Venice in late May – it rotates between the towns (Pisa, Venice, Genoa and Amalfi) who compete in this grand procession and boat race.

WHAT'S HOT…/WHAT'S NOT…

Hot: living with your parents well into your 30s.
Not: families with more than one child.
The two facts *are* related.

HOT TOPIC OF THE DAY

Silvio Berlusconi: whether he manages to cling on as Prime Minister or not, the maverick media-magnate is always a fascinating topic. Has he managed to ride out the scandals?

RANDOM FACTS

✪ Italy has had 62 governments in the 66 years since WWII.

✪ Despite being a Catholic country, Italy has one of the lowest birthrates in Europe, at 1.31 children per family.

✪ In Italy it's possible to buy a property *nuda proprietà* (bare ownership), which usually means the apartment/house still has a resident elderly person. The buyer can't take possession until the person dies: the older they are, the more expensive the property is.

MOST BIZARRE SIGHT

I Vattienti takes place every Easter Saturday in Nocera Torinese, a small town in Calabria. During this solemn procession penitents, wearing black shorts rolled up so high they look like hot pants, beat their bare legs with glass-studded cork until the street runs with their blood. This they do to bring themselves closer to the Passion of Christ, and to assuage any wrongdoings – the prevalence of the 'Ndrangheta (Mafia) in this region may have something to do with the ritual's popularity.

'So you think you've seen it all? We're betting Tanzania still has a surprise or two for you.'

○ TANZANIA

By Paula Hardy

08

TANZANIA

- ○ **POPULATION** 41 MILLION
- ○ **VISITORS PER YEAR** 640,000
- ○ **CAPITAL** DODOMA
- ○ **LANGUAGES** KISWAHILI (OR SWAHILI), KIUNGUJA, ENGLISH, ARABIC
- ○ **MAJOR INDUSTRY** AGRICULTURE AND AGRICULTURAL PROCESSING
- ○ **UNIT OF CURRENCY** TANZANIAN SHILLING (TSH)
- ○ **COST INDEX** MIDRANGE SAFARI PER PERSON PER DAY TSH270,500 (US$200), 1L OF WATER TSH500 (US$0.40), SERENGETI NATIONAL PARK ENTRY TSH70,000 (US$50), STREET SNACK OR PAPAYA TSH200 (US$0.15), SHORT TAXI RIDE TSH2000 (US$1.50)

MARK DAFFEY » LPI

SAFARI SECRETS

It's true, Tanzania is a place of great marvels – Serengeti, Ngorongoro, Kilimanjaro, Zanzibar... The names slip off the tongue like a roll call of Africa's most alluring destinations. But that's not all. It also has great herds of elephants in Ruaha, tree-climbing lions around Lake Manyara, chimpanzee sanctuaries in Gombe and Mahale and packs of wild dogs in Selous. There are also sunsets on the Rufiji River, when the water boils with hippos and crocodiles. In fact, the country has the whole panoply of east Africa's wildlife – including such rarities as the red colobus monkey, black rhino, hawksbill and leatherback turtles and Pemba flying foxes – concentrated in an unrivalled collection of parks and reserves. So you think you've seen it all? We're betting Tanzania still has a surprise or two for you.

CORAL & ECOLOGY

Whoever said tourism and responsible environmental management couldn't go hand-in-hand has never been to Chumbe Island Coral Park. Situated about 12km south of Zanzibar Town, this pristine coral reef is the site of Tanzania's most impressive ecotourism initiative. It's so good that it has received international acclaim from the UN for its impressive non-profit work in protecting the reef, running community outreach initiatives and responsibly managed tourism. It can be visited as a day trip, but if you can, stay in one of the seven ecobungalows to give yourself time to enjoy more than 200 species of coral, 370 species of fish, friendly dolphins and rare hawksbill turtles.

DEFINING EXPERIENCE

After trekking along the knife edge of Mt Meru's crater rim, chasing chimpanzees in the Mahale mountains and tracking wild dogs in Selous, put your feet up on the MV *Liemba* and cruise across Lake Tanganyika – the world's longest lake – before finishing up with a session of *taarab* (traditional) music at the Culture Musical Club on Zanzibar.

RECENT FAD

Capitalism. Throughout the '70s, '80s and '90s Tanzania was famous as Africa's Great Socialist Experiment. However, while President Nyerere's policies of collective farming and *ujamaa* (familyhood) helped form a strong Tanzanian identity, they plunged the country into economic crisis. Since the year 2000 the country has adopted a more capitalist approach, which luckily for tourists has meant a gradual improvement in infrastructure, easier currency exchange and in general a more outward looking nation.

FESTIVALS & EVENTS

✪ Getting tired of the London and New York marathons? Try running the Kilimanjaro Marathon instead. It's scheduled for 27 February in 2011 and starts and finishes in Moshi.

✪ Measure the country's artistic pulse at the Festival of the Dhow Countries, held in mid-July. It's East Africa's largest film and arts festival, with artists from various Indian Ocean Rim countries gathering to enjoy two weeks of dance, music, film and literature.

LIFE-CHANGING EXPERIENCES

✪ Viewing vast herds of game in one of the earth's largest volcanic craters, the Ngorongoro, as shafts of sunlight break through the clouds in a 'Dawn of Time' moment.

ARIADNE VAN ZANDBERGEN » LPI

✪ Paddling through gorgeous riverine scenery on the Rufiji seeking heart-stopping encounters with hippopotamuses.

✪ Getting acquainted with the underwater wonderworld of Mafia island with its technicolour coral, green and hawksbill turtles and seasonal whale sharks.

RANDOM FACTS

✪ DNA lineages found in Tanzania are among the oldest in the world, making the country a strong contender for distinction as the 'cradle of humanity'.

✪ Julius Nyerere (1922–1999), Father of the Nation and the first president of Tanzania, is one of only nine African presidents to relinquish power voluntarily.

✪ Since they were first measured in the early 20th century, Kilimanjaro's glaciers have lost more than 80% of their ice and it is estimated that they will disappear completely by 2020.

✪ The Great Rift Valley, which scores through Tanzania, is a massive geological fault stretching 6500km, all the way from the Dead Sea to Beira (Mozambique).

✪ During the birthing season (February) in the Serengeti over 8000 wildebeest calves are born each day.

MOST BIZARRE SIGHT

Fitting your own young feet into the 3.75-million-year-old fossilised footprints of our oldest known hominid ancestors at Laetoli in the Olduvai Gorge.

'Out east the Bedouin still herd their scraggly sheep and welcome strangers into goat-hair tents for tea.'

By Jessica Lee

09

SYRIA

- ✪ **POPULATION** 21.7 MILLION
- ✪ **FOREIGN VISITORS PER YEAR** 6 MILLION (MORE THAN HALF FROM NEIGHBOURING ARAB COUNTRIES)
- ✪ **CAPITAL** DAMASCUS
- ✪ **LANGUAGES** ARABIC (OFFICIAL), KURDISH, ARAMAIC
- ✪ **MAJOR INDUSTRIES** OIL, TEXTILES, TOBACCO, PHOSPHATE ROCK MINING
- ✪ **UNIT OF CURRENCY** SYRIAN POUND (SYP)
- ✪ **COST INDEX** MIDRANGE HOTEL DOUBLE ROOM SYP1880–2580 (US$40–55), FALAFEL SANDWICH SYP50 (US$1), BUS FROM DAMASCUS TO ALEPPO SYP200 (US$4)

WAYNE WALTON » LPI

FROSTY RELATIONS BEGINNING TO THAW

Heard the one about Bashar al-Assad and the US Ambassador? Well it's no joke. After five years of cold-shoulder treatment relations have thawed and Syria is officially off the naughty step. There's a definite upwardly-mobile attitude taking over the streets, thanks in part to the state-controlled economy slowly being overhauled and the noose of the 'Axis of Evil' tag no longer hanging around the nation's neck.

MODERN YET INFINITELY ANCIENT

Savvy tourists can lord it up like a pasha, staying in lovingly restored Ottoman palaces and sipping cappuccino after shopping it up in the souq. But with all this modernisation it's good to see some things are still the same. Out east the Bedouin still herd their scraggly sheep and welcome strangers into goat-hair tents for tea. Aleppo and Damascus' Old Cities remain mazes where the best maps won't work, and the countryside is still a vast open-air museum, strewn with the abandoned playgrounds of fallen empires.

With hospitality still a national obsession, the attitude to visitors hasn't changed either. The Syrian smile has won over many a traveller already and with the leaders of the West now knocking on Syria's door, it looks like the Syrians may have even more to smile about soon.

DEFINING EXPERIENCE

Haggle with the shopkeepers of Damascus' souq as they brew you a cup of syrupy tea and shower you with handfuls of sugar-coated almonds. Then head for the green hills of the Jebel Ansariyya where the Crusader Castle of Crac des Chevaliers supplies ample opportunity for all would-be knights. Finally make the dusty desert journey to the grand remains of the caravan city of Palmyra and watch the sinking sun turn the ruins golden as the evening draws near.

FESTIVALS & EVENTS

✪ Chaos descends on the sleepy desert outpost of Palmyra in May, when the Al-Bayda Festival brings a riot of camel racing and folk dancing to town for four days. The

HOLGER LEUE » LPI

THE GRAND ARCHITECTURE OF THE UMAYYAD MOSQUE IN DAMASCUS INSPIRES THE FAITHFUL festivities come to a close with a bang with the crowning of 'Miss Desert' inside the Temple of Bal.

✪ Big-band and bebop take over the Damascus citadel for July's Jazz Lives in Syria festival for four days of toe-tapping grooves.

✪ Arabic pop-stars, orchestras and folk groups all take centre stage at Bosra's international festival in September with the largest Roman theatre in the Middle East providing a suitably awe-inspiring venue.

LIFE-CHANGING EXPERIENCES

✪ Scrambling through the ravine leading to Deir Mar Musa, the restored monastery boasting panoramic views, colourful frescos and an eclectic band of international monks and nuns.

✪ Losing the will to protect your modesty in the tiled enclave of the hammam and succumbing to the soaping, scrubbing and massaging doled out by your brusque and cackling attendant.

HOT TOPIC OF THE DAY

The influx of Iraqi refugees, who fled here to escape the war across the border, has pushed the country's services to breaking point. The strain of hosting approximately 1.2 million Iraqis has seen basic living costs spiral and property prices rise sharply and left Syria's public healthcare and education systems struggling to find the resources to cope.

RANDOM FACTS

✪ Asma al-Assad (wife to President Bashar) is a Facebook member despite the website being officially banned in Syria by her husband.

✪ Local Damascene legend states that Jesus Christ will return to earth through the southeast corner minaret of the city's Umayyad Mosque. Watch your head if you're standing beside it when Armageddon strikes.

✪ Syria put its first man in space in 1987. Cosmonaut Muhammad Faris was a member of the first visiting crew to the Mir space station as part of a Soviet-Syrian space mission.

MOST BIZARRE SIGHT

If you think standing on a pillar to prove your closeness to God is a bit excessive, then how about staying up on that pillar for another 42 years? That's exactly what St Simeon did, starting off a pillar-topping craze in the early Byzantine world. You can still visit the remnants of one of his pillars, along with the cathedral the Byzantines built around it after his death. With the wind eerily whispering through the remains of the basilica, Qala'at Samaan is one of the most atmospheric outposts to be found in Syria.

'…if Japan has been on your travel wishlist for a while, make this the year that you finally see the birthplace of sushi, sake and sumo.'

By Matthew D Firestone

10

JAPAN

- ✪ **POPULATION** 127 MILLION
- ✪ **FOREIGN VISITORS PER YEAR** 6.8 MILLION
- ✪ **CAPITAL** TOKYO
- ✪ **LANGUAGE** JAPANESE
- ✪ **MAJOR INDUSTRIES** MOTOR VEHICLES, ELECTRONIC EQUIPMENT, MACHINE TOOLS, STEEL AND NONFERROUS METALS, SHIPS, CHEMICALS, TEXTILES, PROCESSED FOODS
- ✪ **UNIT OF CURRENCY** YEN (¥)
- ✪ **COST INDEX** BOWL OF RAMEN NOODLES ¥800 (US$8.50), PINT OF SAPPORO BEER ¥400 (US$4.25), BED IN A CAPSULE HOTEL ¥4000 (US$42.50), CROSS-TOWN TAXI ¥2500 (US$26.50)

DOWN, BUT NOT OUT...

It's been a rough year for the Land of the Rising Sun. Although the Japan National Tourism Organization (JNTO) had hoped to attract 10 million foreign visitors a year by 2010, this lofty target was dropped quicker than a *maegashira* (lowest sumo rank) squaring off against a *yokozuna* (sumo grand champion). The Great Recession, the rapid deflation of the yen against Western currencies and the spread of H1N1 influenza in Asia resulted in the first annual decrease in tourism in more than two decades. Japan may be down, but it's not out. Case in point: the JNTO recently issued a new target of 20 million foreign visitors annually by 2020, which means that now more than ever, travellers touching down in Japan are treated as most honoured guests.

JOHN BANAGAN » LPI

CHERRY BLOSSOM SEASON AT OSAKA CASTLE – BE SURE TO SPRING INTO JAPAN AT THIS MAGICAL TIME OF YEAR

SUSHI, SAKE & SUMO

Japan has an ill-deserved reputation as an expensive destination where the English language is in short supply. But US$100 cuts of Kobe beef and the occasional *Lost in Translation* moment aside, Japan is surprisingly affordable and user-friendly. Before you go, stop by your local travel agency and purchase a Japan Rail Pass, which grants you unlimited access to the country's sophisticated transport network. While Tokyo was ultimately unsuccessful in its bid for the 2016 Summer Olympics, the campaign resulted in increased English signage across the country. So, if Japan has been on your travel wishlist for a while, make this the year that you finally see the birthplace of sushi, sake and sumo.

DEFINING EXPERIENCE

Japan is home to so many travel clichés that every experience you have here will be strangely familiar despite being completely foreign. Race past rice paddies on a lightning-fast bullet train while tucking into a perfectly balanced bento box. Strip down, scrub clean and slowly ease your travel-worn body into a sulphurous hot spring. Sip *matcha* (powdered green tea) as you silently reflect on the flawless perfection of a Zen rock garden. Photograph street parades of teen fashionistas sporting goth Lolita dresses and anime costumes. Slurp down a bowl of al dente ramen noodles floating in a broth of miso, soy sauce and seasoned pork fat. Hike millennia-old foot trails linking together mountaintop Buddhist temples and aesthetic places of worship. The list goes on and on…

FESTIVALS & EVENTS

✪ In January, there is no bigger event than Tokyo's annual Grand Sumo Tournament, a multiday battle between the sport's largest and most celebrated behemoths.

BRENT WINEBRENNER » LPI

☉ In February, head north to the frozen island of Hokkaido for the Sapporo Snow Festival, which is highlighted by an ice sculpture–carving contest.

☉ Late March and early April is a glorious time to be in Japan, especially since the blooming of the *sakura* (cherry blossoms) heralds the springtime.

☉ The historic Asakusa district in Tokyo attracts more than a million people each May for the Sanja Matsuri, a Shinto festival involving a thronging parade of *mikoshi* (portable shrines).

☉ July and August mark the official climbing season for Mt Fuji, the country's iconic volcano that peaks at 3776m. Summer festivals and fireworks displays abound.

☉ Mid-November hosts *Shichi-go-san* (Seven-five-three); parents celebrate these milestone ages by dressing up their children in kimonos and bringing them to shrines.

RANDOM FACTS

☉ The average Japanese person eats more than 60kg of rice per year.

☉ High-quality sake is served chilled, as room temperature or higher will mask the true flavour and aroma.

☉ In 2008 scientists discovered how to raise non-poisonous *fugu* (blowfish) by specially controlling their diet.

☉ The sudden bloom and rapid death of cherry blossoms is an enduring Buddhist symbol for the cycle of life.

☉ Sumo wrestlers bulk up by eating massive quantities of *chankonabe*, a rich stew of fish, meat and vegetables.

☉ Traditional handsewn silk kimonos with accompanying accessories can cost upwards of US$30,000.

☉ In experimental test runs, the bullet train reaches speeds of more than 440 km/h.

052
SINAI

056
ISTRIA

060
MARQUESAS ISLANDS

064
CAPPADOCIA

068
WESTFJORDS

LONELY PLANET'S
TOP 10 REGIONS

'Ecolodges and idyllic beach-hut camps between Taba and Dahab are now attracting travellers looking for a peaceful retreat in the Middle East.

By Dan Savery Raz

01

SINAI, EGYPT

- ✪ **POPULATION** 380,500 (NOT INCLUDING SUEZ CANAL)
- ✪ **MAIN TOWN** SHARM EL-SHEIKH
- ✪ **LANGUAGE** ARABIC
- ✪ **MAJOR INDUSTRY** TOURISM
- ✪ **UNIT OF CURRENCY** EGYPTIAN POUND (E£)
- ✪ **COST INDEX** HOTEL DOUBLE/DORM ROOM FOR A NIGHT E£340/80 (US$62/15), ONE-HOUR TAXI RIDE E£40 (US$7), FULL-DAY SCUBA DIVE E£350 (US$63), PLATE OF *KALAMAARI* E£40 (US$7), SUNSET TOUR FROM DAHAB TO MT SINAI E£120 (US$22)

JANE SWEENEY » LPI

PAINT IT RED

OK, Sharm el-Sheikh is being sold for its cheap winter sun but Sinai is much more than a convenient place for Europeans to top up their tans. Away from the Costa del Camel, this mighty desert peninsula is home to a mystical red-rock mountain range, said to have played a major role in the foundation of the three major monotheistic faiths. The Red Sea's phenomenal coral reef may have brought divers from all over the globe, but in recent years a new type of tourism has emerged. Ecolodges and idyllic beach-hut camps between Taba and Dahab are now attracting travellers looking for a peaceful retreat in the Middle East. President Mubarak's government may have spent much of the past decade developing the 'Red Sea Riviera' with huge hotels and golf resorts but parts of Sinai still have that familiar old hippy-trail vibe.

HOLY MOSES!

Every day thousands of people make the pilgrimage to a remote, barren valley in the middle of Sinai to climb the mountain where it is said Moses had a one-to-one with God. Whatever your beliefs, there is no denying the majestic views from Mt Sinai. At dawn or dusk, the summit of this mighty mount is the Holy Grail for panoramic photographs. On your ascent or descent, be sure to visit St Katherine's Monastery, which was founded in around AD 330 by the Roman Empress Helena. Today, about 20 Greek Orthodox monks live in the monastery, assisted by Bedouins and Muslims of the Jebeliyah tribe. Don't miss the amazing Monastery Museum, home to some of the oldest books on earth including part of the Codex Sinaiticus, Christianity's earliest New Testament. Thou shalt not be disappointed.

DEFINING EXPERIENCE

Explore one of the world's most beautiful coral reefs at the Ras Abu Gallum Protectorate, then take a camel trek to Coloured Canyon and learn the true meaning of 'psychedelic rock'. The next day climb Mt Sinai at dawn, then spend the rest of the day

MARK DAFFEY » LPI

SO THAT'S WHERE THOSE LITTLE COCKTAIL UMBRELLAS COME FROM! SHARM EL-SHEIKH TURNS ON THE CHARM

lazing on a hammock on the sand-dune beaches of Tarabin and at night recline with a
sheesha pipe on the shores of the Red Sea.

THE GREEN SCENE

Way before the terms 'ecotourism' and 'green tourism' were bandied around,
the Bedouin of Sinai were using sustainable building methods along the Red Sea
coast. Started in 1982, Basata, which means 'simplicity' in Arabic, is Egypt's first
ecolodge. Consisting of bamboo huts and mud-brick chalets, the camp uses only
organic produce, recycles all its rubbish and is now one of the best-known camps in
the region. And the green idea seems to be catching on. Inland in the St Katherine
Protectorate lies the more remote ecolodge Al-Karm, built on an ancient Nabatean
settlement. Even in Dahab, local businesses such as Desert Divers are starting to run
beach and coral reef clean-ups for conscientious campers.

FESTIVALS & EVENTS

✪ Forget bunnies and chocolate eggs; instead celebrate Easter in April at St
Katherine's, the world's oldest functioning Christian monastery.

✪ Running a marathon in the desert may sound like lunacy, but that's exactly what
you can do in November at the SharMarathon. Held at Ras Mohammed National
Park, the sand dunes, red rock mountains and turquoise waters make for an inspiring
backdrop.

✪ Sharm el-Sheikh's Old Market comes alive with four days of fireworks, parades and
DJs at the Sharm International Carnival in December.

RANDOM FACTS

✪ Sinai is the only part of Egypt located in Asia and not Africa.

✪ Although the Suez Canal was opened in 1869, the legendary Egyptian Pharaoh
Sesostris began work on a similar canal almost 3800 years earlier in 1897 BC.

✪ According to the famous English archaeologist Flinders Petrie, the number of people
that left Egypt in the Exodus was 27,000, not three million as has been suggested
elsewhere.

✪ A natural habitat for rare species of fish and more than 200 types of coral, the Red
Sea is the world's northernmost tropical sea.

DEFINING DIFFERENCE

Sinai feels like a separate state. Geographically it is disconnected from the rest of Egypt
by the Suez and from the rest of Arabia by the Red Sea, and it is a place for healing and
relaxation. Where else in Egypt can you find camps with Buddhist names like Shanti
and Nirvana or take beachfront yoga lessons? After the chaos of Cairo, the Red Sea's
aqua-blue waters force you to slow down and get some well-needed 'me' time.

'Blessed with a year-round mild climate, Istria packs a dazzling diversity of landscapes and experiences into a small triangular shape…'

By Anja Mutić

ISTRIA, CROATIA

- ✪ **POPULATION** 206,000
- ✪ **MAIN TOWN** PULA
- ✪ **LANGUAGES** CROATIAN (OFFICIAL), ITALIAN (UNOFFICIAL)
- ✪ **UNIT OF CURRENCY** CROATIAN KUNA (KN)
- ✪ **MAJOR INDUSTRIES** PROCESSING INDUSTRIES (SHIPBUILDING, CONSTRUCTION, TEXTILE), TOURISM, TRADE
- ✪ **COST INDEX** A DISH WITH TRUFFLES 145KN (US$27), ONE NIGHT AT AN AGROTURIZAM PER PERSON 200KN (US$38), 1L OF WINE 15-30KN (US$2.80-$5.60)

ART, FOOD, WINE & MAGIC

Tone Tuscany down a notch or two – thin the tourist hordes, lower the prices, sprinkle a little mystique – and you get Istria. Shaped like a heart, this Italian-flavoured peninsula of 3600 sq km is where continental Croatia meets the Adriatic. In summer months, the sun-and-sea set storms the resort-lined coast, or so-called 'blue Istria'. For art, food, wine and an offbeat vibe, head to the interior, nicknamed 'green Istria' – a bucolic dream of rolling hills, hilltop villages, rural B&Bs and farmhouse restaurants.

FROM TRUFFLES TO DINOSAURS

Blessed with a year-round mild climate, Istria packs a dazzling diversity of landscapes and experiences into a small triangular shape – from dinosaur footprints, Roman amphitheatres and Byzantine basilicas to deep-green fjords and subterranean chambers. The usual Mediterranean trimmings grace the Adriatic coastline – crystal-clear seas, pebble beaches, verdant parklands and historic seaside towns. Istria's interior packs even more of a punch: a land of vineyard-covered hills, olive groves, asparagus-dotted meadows, truffle-rich forests, medieval settlements and quirky hamlets.

WAYNE WALTON » LPI

HANG WITH SOME HOTTIES IN ISTRIA

DEFINING EXPERIENCE

Spend the morning hours exploring the wild landscapes and virgin beaches of Rt Kamenjak cape. Next tour Pula's Roman amphitheatre for a spot of history, then hit the road for a winding, adventurous ride through the interior of Istria to discover ancient hill towns. Finally, finish off the day with a truffle-based meal at a traditional tavern.

FESTIVALS & EVENTS

✪ Every July and August, the artsy town of Labin, perched on a hill in Istria's interior, comes alive for Labin Art Republic, when more than 30 resident artists open their studios and streets buzz with outdoor theatre, concerts and clown performances.

✪ Celebrate the start of the white truffle season in the sleepy cobblestone town of Buzet, where the festival of Subotina on the second Saturday in September centres on the preparation of a giant truffle omelette (with more than 2000 eggs and 10kg of truffles) in a 1000kg pan.

✪ Work on your groovy moves every July at the Festival of Dance & Nonverbal Theatre in the Renaissance-flavoured town of Svetvinčenat. Performances range from Finnish hop-hop and circus acts to Brazilian capoeira.

✪ Hip international film buffs descend on the hilltop town of Motovun every summer in late July/early August for the Motovun Film Festival, known for its alfresco and indoor screenings of independent and avant-garde films, concerts and parties, set against the town's striking medieval backdrop.

LIFE-CHANGING EXPERIENCES

✪ Hunting for prized white truffles in the forests around Buzet and Motovun, and then feasting on the fragrant fungus at Stara Oštarija restaurant in Buzet, where even ice cream comes with olive oil and truffles.

✪ Exploring the Rovinj archipelago of 13 small verdant islands in a sea kayak, visiting lighthouses and lunching at pretty islets.

✪ Spending a holiday on a family farm in Istria's interior. Try Agroturizam Ograde, a rural hideaway where you can feast on wholesome food, help out with the animals, and hike and bike in the scenic surroundings.

WHAT'S HOT...

✪ Off-season weekend escapes to Brijuni National Park, the former playground of Yugoslavia's jet-setting ex-president Tito, where the main island's hotels showcase serious communist chic with their utilitarian look and feel.

✪ Wine and olive oil tastings are the region's latest fad. Sip on Croatia's top wines in the cellars of Istria's winemakers, and savour award-winning olive oil varieties in select restaurants. With your own wheels, you can follow routes that centre on wine

WITOLD SKRYPCZAK » LPI

and olive oil, visiting vineyards and olive groves, and tasting these nectars right from the source.

✪ Lighthouse retreats, all the rage along the Croatian coast, require booking far in advance. Stay at Savudrija, the oldest lighthouse in the Adriatic and the northernmost in Croatia, built in 1818 by an Austrian count for a beautiful Croatian lady.

REGIONAL FLAVOURS

Up and coming as a veritable foodie heaven, Istria is known for its gastronomic tradition that features fresh foodstuffs (like wild asparagus and white truffles), unique dishes and prime wines. Look out for the following yummy specialties: *maneštra,* a thick vegetable-and-bean soup similar to minestrone; *fuži,* hand-rolled pasta often served with *tartufi* (truffles picked in autumn) or *divljač* (game meat); *fritaja,* omelette often served with seasonal vegies, such as wild asparagus harvested in spring; and thin slices of dry-cured Istrian *pršut* (ham).

'…the Marquesas still feel like the world's end.
Here, nature's fingers have sculpted intricate jewels
that jut dramatically from the Pacific Ocean.'

MARQUESAS ISLANDS ✪

By Jean-Bernard Carillet

03

MARQUESAS ISLANDS, FRENCH POLYNESIA

- ✪ **POPULATION** 8000
- ✪ **MAIN TOWN** TAIOHAE
- ✪ **LANGUAGES** FRENCH, MARQUESAN
- ✪ **MAJOR INDUSTRIES** AGRICULTURE, TOURISM
- ✪ **UNIT OF CURRENCY** PACIFIC FRANC (CFP)
- ✪ **COST INDEX** GLASS OF BEER 400CFP (US$4.55), B&B DOUBLE ROOM 8000CFP (US$91), 4WD EXCURSION 10,000CFP (US$114), SMALL *TIKI* WOODEN SCUPLTURE 8000CFP (US$91)

JEAN-BERNARD CARILLET » LPI

PARADISE LOST

The famous French painter Paul Gauguin didn't escape to the Marquesas for nothing. Constantly in search of a place to eschew civilisation and find perfection, he finally settled in the Marquesas in 1901. He couldn't have picked a better place. About 1500km northeast of Tahiti, the Marquesas still feel like the world's end. Here, nature's fingers have sculpted intricate jewels that jut dramatically from the Pacific Ocean. Waterfalls taller than skyscrapers trickle down vertical canyons, the ocean thrashes at towering sea cliffs, sharp basalt pinnacles project from emerald forests and scalloped bays are blanketed with desert arcs of white or black sand. The Marquesans live in a sprinkling of tiny villages where time moves at a crawl.

NATURE & CULTURE

Nature is not the only drawcard. In everything from cuisine and dance to language and crafts, the Marquesas feel different from the rest of French Polynesia. Despite the trappings of the modern world (internet, mobile phones), the people residing here are adamantly tied to their traditions. The archipelago also makes for a mind-boggling museum, with plenty of sites dating from pre-European times, all shrouded with a palpable historical aura.

PETER HENDRIE » LPI

2011 – WHEN THE MARQUESAS GO WILD

Powerful, grandiose, visceral – words do little justice to the Marquesas Arts Festival, French Polynesia's premier festival, which lasts about one week and is held once every four years, usually in December, on one of the three bigger Marquesas Islands (Nuku Hiva, Hiva Oa or Ua Pou). It's so impressive that it's worth timing your trip around it. The next edition is due on Nuku Hiva in December 2011 – book your flight now!

What can you expect? The festival revolves around a series of dance and cultural contests. Groups from all the Marquesas Islands demonstrate their skills at traditional dances, including the spine-tingling Haka Manu (Dance of the Bird) and Haka Pua (Dance of the Pig). Most dancing contests take place at archaeological sites – huge platforms of stone blocks in the jungle – which provide an incredibly atmospheric stage. Events also include traditional Marquesan meal preparations as well as arts and crafts displays.

DEFINING EXPERIENCE

Don your explorer's hat and live out your Indiana Jones fantasies while wandering amid enigmatic *tiki* (sacred sculptures), petroglyphs and sacred sites hidden in the jungle, then experience timeless traditional village life on Ua Huka or Ua Pou, meeting master carvers and tattoo artists.

FESTIVALS & EVENTS

✪ The Marquesas Arts Festival is an incredibly colourful, week-long celebration of Marquesan identity and is held once every four years in December. It's your top chance to immerse yourself in some traditional Marquesan culture. Earmark December 2011.

✪ If you don't have the patience to wait until December 2011 or 2015, 'mini festivals' are held on the smaller islands (Fatu Hiva, Ua Huka) in between the 'big' festivals.

LIFE-CHANGING EXPERIENCES

✪ Gazing down impenetrable valleys while hiking across the Nuku Hiva or Hiva Oa heartlands.

✪ Clip-clopping across Hiva Oa's fecund interior.

✪ Experiencing the thrills of snorkelling alongside (harmless) whale sharks off Nuka Hiva.

HOT TOPIC OF THE DAY

The *Aranui*. This 104m boat is the umbilical cord between Tahiti and the Marquesas and has been supplying the six inhabited islands of the archipelago since 1984. It also doubles as a cruise ship for tourists. The loading and unloading of freight is always a major event on the islands.

MOST BIZARRE SIGHT

Jojo, Jacques Brel's plane, in the town of Atuona, on Hiva Oa. Like Gauguin, Belgian-born singer-songwriter Jacques Brel also chose to live out his life on Hiva Oa. He equipped himself with *Jojo*, a Beechcraft aeroplane in which he travelled between the main islands and performed medical evacuations to Tahiti.

DEFINING DIFFERENCE

Tranquil lagoons and swanky resorts, as in Bora Bora? Oh no, no. Unlike other islands in French Polynesia, the Marquesas are devoid of barrier-reef and protective lagoons; the feeling here is wild and earthbound. With only a smattering of B&Bs and just two hotels, they're rather an ecotourist's dream.

LOCAL LINGO

The Marquesan language is surprisingly different from Tahitian. In fact, it's closer to the Maori spoken in New Zealand. A little effort with some simple words will be greatly appreciated by the local people. Try *kaoha* (hello), *apae* (goodbye) and *koutou* (thank you).

'If you want to live like a troglodyte, you should rock 'n' roll to Turkey now, before Cappadocia is changed forever.'

By James Bainbridge

CAPPADOCIA, TURKEY

- ✪ **POPULATION** 350,000
- ✪ **MAIN TOWN** NEVŞEHIR
- ✪ **LANGUAGE** TURKISH
- ✪ **MAJOR INDUSTRY** TOURISM
- ✪ **UNIT OF CURRENCY** TÜRK LIRASI (TL, TURKISH LIRA)
- ✪ **COST INDEX** BUS TO İSTANBUL TL50/US$33, UNDERGROUND CITY ENTRANCE TL15/US$10, DOUBLE ROOM/CAVE DORM WITH BREAKFAST TL78/25 (US$51/16), TWO-HOUR HORSE RIDE TL50/US$33

WIND OF CHANGE

With the slow pace of life in its villages, it seems like Cappadocia sees little change other than winds eroding the fairy chimneys (rock formations). However, as surely as Mt Erciyes towers in the distance, the modern world is encroaching here. If you want to live like a troglodyte, you should rock 'n' roll to Turkey now, before Cappadocia is changed forever.

Conservation efforts are made, but coach parties keep arriving. More and more hot-air balloons dot the sky on summer mornings, and the allure of tourist dosh is proving great in an area once devoted to agriculture. The pigeon houses on the rock faces, traditionally used to collect bird droppings for use as fertiliser, increasingly lie empty.

But Cappadocia is still worth the trek from İstanbul. Once you've left Göreme's Flintstones-referencing backpacker joints behind, and hiked into the valleys of wavy white rock, the 21st century feels like a distant world.

DEFINING EXPERIENCE

Bound out of your fairy chimney before the sun rises over the knobbly landscape to see it all from above on a dawn hot-air balloon ride. Back on terra firma, resist the temptation of a Cloud 9 cocktail and head along the quiet country roads to Soğanlı or Ihlara Valley, where Byzantine monks carved churches into the cliffs. For some respite from the Anatolian sun, disappear into the subterranean cities where Byzantine Christians hid from Persian and Arabic armies. Crown the day with a wander through the valleys, and a long look at sunset from a panoramic restaurant terrace.

MARK AVELLINO » LPI

TALK OF CAPPADOCIA'S AMAZING SCENERY AIN'T ALL HOT AIR

TOP-END CAVES

Cappadocia was once a classic backpacker hangout – a few free spirits have even swapped their rucksack for a fairy chimney home. However, it is becoming more of a midrange and top-end destination, and the accommodation reflects this. In the summer, daily flights between İstanbul and both Nevşehir and Kayseri, and regular flights between the latter and İzmir, enable folk with cash to jet between the must-sees.

PILGRIMS, POTS & PLONK

✪ From 16 to 18 August, thousands of Hacı Bektaş Veli devotees pay their respects at the 13th-century dervish's tomb, in Hacıbektaş. After politicians have said their bit, two days of music, dance and superstitious rites ensue.

✪ The Avanos Handicrafts Festival, at the end of August in 2011, celebrates the town's main industry: pottery, made with red clay from its river.

✪ Cappadocia's fertile volcanic soil has long produced wine; Ürgüp's International Wine Festival raises a glass to the grape harvest in early October.

PHIL WEYMOUTH » LPI

TURKEY'S WHIRLING DERVISH CEREMONIES WILL HAVE YOUR HEAD SPINNING

WHAT'S HOT...
Hot-air balloons and boutique fairy chimneys.

WHAT'S NOT...
Dossing in a musty cave and subsisting on local apricots.

KAMIKAZE JACUZZIS
Central Anatolia suffers from desertification and a water shortage, yet Cappadocia's accommodation owners keep installing jacuzzis and pools. Water has even been trucked to Göreme, which has about 100 hotels, hostels and pensions, from nearby villages. A recently introduced water system, whereby locals top up their accounts by paying at the *belediye* (town hall), is hoped to alleviate the problem. The municipal council also plans to tear down Göreme's wooden kiosk restaurants and move the *otogar* (bus station) to make room for a car park, signalling that tourism threatens to spoil much more than the village's sedate atmosphere.

RANDOM FACTS
✪ Cappadocia's fairy chimneys and curvy valleys are made of tuff – compressed volcanic ash, from the eruption of Mt Erciyes.

✪ In Cappadocia's agricultural past, if a man didn't own a pigeon house, he would struggle to woo a wife.

✪ Visitors can watch whirling dervish ceremonies in the 13th-century Sarıhan caravanserai.

IMAGINATION VALLEY
The fantastic fairy chimneys in this area, which more prosaic locals call Devrent Valley, resemble everything from Napoleon's hat to a couple of kissing birds.

CAPPADOCIAN CHARACTERS
Since Christians sought refuge here between the 4th and 11th centuries, Cappadocia has been a distinct area. Its inhabitants are proud of the rural lives they lead in this unique setting, although the modern world is eroding traditions. Tourism has introduced some commercialisation, but the touts lack their İstanbul cohorts' persistence; if you don't buy that carpet, they will happily drink yet more *çay* (tea) and gaze at the fairy chimneys.

TROGLODYTE FARE
Cappadocia is a great place to try a dramatic central Anatolian speciality, *testi kebap* (pottery kebab). Meat or mushrooms, as well as vegetables, are cooked in a sealed terracotta pot, which is broken at the table. If the restaurant slow-cooks the dish in the traditional manner, you must order three hours before eating.

⊙ WESTFJORDS

EUROPE

NORTH AMERICA

ASIA

AMERICA

AUSTRALIA

'The Westfjords are home to one of Europe's largest and finest remaining wilderness areas, and much of this land is vast, empty and beautiful open space…'

By Tom Hall

WESTFJORDS, ICELAND

- ✪ **POPULATION** 7300
- ✪ **MAIN TOWN** ÍSAFJÖRDUR
- ✪ **LANGUAGE** ICELANDIC
- ✪ **MAJOR INDUSTRIES** FISHERIES, TOURISM
- ✪ **UNIT OF CURRENCY** ICELANDIC KRÓNA (IKR)

✪ **COST INDEX** CUP OF COFFEE IKR300 (US$2.40), MIDRANGE HOTEL DOUBLE IKR16,000 (US$127), SHORT TAXI RIDE IKR4000 (US$32), INTERNET ACCESS – NORMALLY FREE, OTHERWISE PER HOUR IKR100 (US$0.80)

FRANS LEMMENS » LPI

ICELAND'S WILD WEST

Anyone lucky enough to visit Iceland comes back goggle-eyed and open-jawed with tales of an untamed island of volcanoes (yes, including *that* volcano), waterfalls and unrivalled natural scenery. Unsurprisingly, routes out of Reykjavík and the circuit of the island are well-trodden, especially in summer months. But there is another Iceland: a quiet whisper about a secret and overlooked corner of the country is becoming a clamour that this year might be too hard to ignore. The place is the Westfjords, that oddly shaped peninsula only just connected to the rest of Iceland by a narrow isthmus of land. It's as isolated as it is spectacular.

NATURE & NOISE

The Westfjords are home to one of Europe's largest and finest remaining wilderness areas, and much of this land is vast, empty and beautiful open space with fjords, mountains, rivers and lakes. But this doesn't mean it's all about nature here. Ísafjördur, the main town, hosts Iceland's best music festival as well as being home to a great local cafe and dining scene. There are surprises out on the road too: the Simbahöllin Café in Thingeyri cooks up mean Belgian waffles, and you'll find hot pools all over the peninsula.

SPECTACULAR JOURNEYS

You can reach Ísafjördur by bus from Reykjavík, and the service runs on two routes: one via Stykkishólmur and the ferry over to Brjánslækur, and one overland via Hólmavík. Once here though, unless relying on boats to get you to the nationally revered Hornstrandir Nature Reserve you need a car to get around. With a vehicle you're free to cruise over high mountain passes and past blue-water fjords.

DEFINING EXPERIENCE

Leave the road, town, cottage and anything else of the artificial world behind and head to the unbeatable Hornstrandir Nature Reserve. This peninsula, uninhabited since 1975, is a magnet for hikers exploring towering cliffs, and classic lake and valley scenery. This is a wild land of unmarked trails and rivers without bridges, so come prepared for adventure and self-sufficiency. In summer boats run from Ísafjördur to a variety of starting points.

RECENT FAD

Bringing it all back home is the big thing, not just in the Westfjords but throughout Iceland. Partly spurred by the economic problems of two years ago and partly by local pride there has been a return to a do-it-yourself ethic, expressed in everything from growing and using local produce in restaurants to a rejuvenation of local arts and crafts.

FESTIVALS & EVENTS

If only all music festivals could be like Aldrei fór ég suður in April. For starters, it's free and aimed as much at children as adults. No act, whether local favourite or international big name, is paid to play or gets more than 20 minutes, and some gigs take place in the local swimming baths in Ísafjördur. The festival is held during ski week.

RICHARD CUMMINS » LPI

LIFE-CHANGING EXPERIENCES

✪ Soaking off a hard-day's hiking, skiing or kayaking in a hot natural pool. You'll find them dotted around the Westfjords.

✪ Wild-camping on deserted golden-sand beaches en route to the Látrabjarg bird cliffs, which from June to August form Europe's largest bird colony.

RANDOM FACTS

✪ The Westfjords village of Flókalundur is named after Flóki Vilgerðarson, the Viking explorer who first dubbed the island Iceland, who passed this way in AD 860.

✪ In 1920 the population of the Westfjords was more than 13,000 – almost twice what it is today. Now the 7300 fiercely proud inhabitants make up just over 2% of Iceland's population.

MOST BIZARRE SIGHT

On the first weekend in August Ísafjördur hosts the European Swamp Soccer Championships. This feast of sliding, falling and splashing about in boggy mud while trying to play football is one of the world's great stupid sports. If you lack enough mad mates to form a team the organisers can usually attach you to a participating side.

DEFINING DIFFERENCE

The Westfjords populace know they're on to a good thing, and see themselves as a place apart from the rest of Iceland. The Aldrei festival's name means 'I never went south', and is a badge of pride for locals who resist the call to relocate to Reykjavík. You'll get to know this fierce pride the longer you stay and the more locals you chat to. They're Westfjorders first, and Icelanders second.

○ SHETLAND ISLANDS

EUROPE

NORTH AMERICA

ASIA

AFRICA

SOUTH AMERICA

AUSTRALIA

'…the Shetlands are a place apart. This might just be the last untamed corner of the United Kingdom.'

By Tom Hall

06

SHETLAND ISLANDS, SCOTLAND

○ **POPULATION** 22,000

○ **MAIN TOWN** LERWICK

○ **LANGUAGE** ENGLISH

○ **MAJOR INDUSTRIES** OIL, FISHERIES, TOURISM

○ **UNIT OF CURRENCY** POUND STERLING (£)

○ **COST INDEX** CUP OF COFFEE £1.50 (US$2.30), MIDRANGE HOTEL DOUBLE IN LERWICK £65 (US$100) – LESS OUTSIDE THE CAPITAL, THREE-HOUR SEABIRD AND SEAL-SPOTTING CRUISE £35–40 (US$54–61), BIKE HIRE PER DAY £7.50 (US$11.50)

TBK » IMAGEBROKER

BRITAIN'S LAST WILDERNESS

Unst, Fetlar and Foula don't sound very British, or indeed Scottish. But they are some of the many islands that make up the little-known Shetland Islands. Part of the UK but closer to Norway than the islands of Great Britain, part of Scotland but less than 100km from Caledonia's north coast, the Shetlands are a place apart. This might just be the last untamed corner of the United Kingdom.

REMOTE, OBSCURE, ESSENTIAL

Shetland Islanders, a fiercely independent and self-reliant bunch, are turning remoteness – it takes some effort to get here – and obscurity to their advantage. Orcas, otters, seals and puffins are easy to spot and you'll often have them all to yourself. There's Bronze Age, Viking and WWII history in abundance. When it comes to walking or off-road biking there are the highest sea cliffs in Europe to discover and weeks of wandering among sparsely-populated islands. Exploring is easy due to a superb oil-funded infrastructure and efficient ferries. And no-one you know has ever been.

ADVENTUROUS TRAVELLERS STEP THIS WAY

2011 looks set to be a record-breaking year for visitor numbers to the archipelago. Lerwick has become a must-include port of call for cruise ships, with 50 vessels having called during the 2010 season, and this year they're joined by the eye-catching vessels of the Tall Ships Race. It's not just nature either: a landmark film and concert venue in Lerwick is set to change the face of the capital's quayside.

DEFINING EXPERIENCE

After a close-up wildlife encounter at the puffin colony at Sumburgh Head, take some time to learn about the Shetland Bus – the clandestine wartime boat service smuggling men and weapons between Shetland and Norway – at the Scalloway Museum. Finish off with a pint of White Wife from Valhalla Brewery on Unst, the UK's most northerly ale producer, handcrafted with local water and loving care.

RECENT FAD

The BBC program *Simon King's Shetland Diaries* has really blown the lid on the islands as a wildlife hotspot. Wildlife filmmaker Simon King spent a year on the islands with his family. His enthusiastic account of his time here delighted locals, while anyone who viewed it would have a hard time not wanting to become one.

HOLGER LEUE » LPI

ISLAND LIFE ON THE SHETLANDS MIGHT PROVIDE THE BREATH OF FRESH AIR YOU NEED

FESTIVALS & EVENTS

✪ Up Helly Aa is a spectacular torchlit parade that celebrates islanders' Norse heritage on the last Tuesday in January. Squads of locals dressed as Vikings and carrying blazing torches parade a longboat through the streets of Lerwick. On arrival at the burning site the torches are thrown into the longboat, setting it alight. If you miss the one in Lerwick there are other similar celebrations in other towns at different times.

✪ Shetland Folk Festival is an annual event held each April bringing the traditional music world to venues across the islands as well as showcasing local talent. One journalist who attended noted 'sleep ranks low on the Shetland priority list' – you have been warned.

✪ July 2011 brings the Tall Ships Race to Lerwick and various guest harbours around the island. The last visit of the race in 1999 was one big party, and July is a wonderful time to visit.

HOT TOPIC OF THE DAY

It may have caused much local debate, but it all promises to be worth it. Opening in 2011, Mareel is a new film and music centre in a striking modern building on Lerwick's quayside, next to the Shetland Museum.

RANDOM FACTS

✪ Shetland Islanders have a long history of friendly rivalry with Orcadians, as natives of the Orkney Islands to the south are known.

✪ The diminutive Shetland pony is native to the islands. Some of them have been trained to act as guide horses, similar to guide dogs, because of their longer life expectancy.

MOST BIZARRE SIGHT

Between Baltasound and Haroldswick on Unst you will find the only fully furnished bus stop in the UK. Local residents deck it out each year to a different theme. Sometimes the shelter becomes a miniature sitting room with a comfy chair, sofa and TV. It has been the UK's smallest cinema and has been decorated in pink to raise funds for breast cancer. It's just the place to sit while you wait for one of the three daily buses that pass along this way.

REGIONAL FLAVOURS

Shetland produces exceptional fish and shellfish, and is also noted for unusual dishes like seawater oatcakes and Shetland black potatoes. All of Britain is falling in love with rhubarb again and Shetland produces a fine variety – try it with mackerel or herring to best combine flavours.

'Staying on a Whitsunday isle is one of the best options for experiencing the reef. There are 74 islands in total but only eight are inhabited…'

○ GREAT BARRIER REEF & WHITSUNDAY ISLANDS

By Rowan Roebig

07

GREAT BARRIER REEF & WHITSUNDAY ISLANDS, AUSTRALIA

✪ **MAIN TOWN/POPULATION** THE MAIN JUMPING-OFF POINT, AIRLIE BEACH, HAS 5000 RESIDENTS

✪ **LANGUAGE** ENGLISH

✪ **MAJOR INDUSTRY** TOURISM

✪ **UNIT OF CURRENCY** AUSTRALIAN DOLLAR (A$)

✪ **COST INDEX** GLASS ('POT') OF XXXX BEER A$3.50 (US$3.25), AIRLIE BEACH HOSTEL DORM/HOTEL ROOM A$25/150 (US$23/139), INTERNET ACCESS PER HOUR A$4 (US$3.70), DAY TRIP TO THE OUTER REEF A$195 (US$180), WITH SCUBA DIVING A$310 (US$287)

WILL THE REEF SURVIVE?

In the short term, yes, but it's uncertain for how long. Around 19% of global coral reefs are already effectively dead and 35% seriously under threat due to a combination of damaging fishing practices, coastal run-off (eg polluted rivers flowing into oceans) and climate change. Growth rates of some coral species in the Great Barrier Reef have declined by 14% over the past 20 years due to temperature stress or ocean acidification. Some studies suggest the reef will be 95% dead by 2050.

It's not all bad news. Responsible snorkelling and scuba diving around the reefs have very little to no damaging effect, and your tourist dollars can contribute to the Barrier Reef's survival. Most major tours here include an 'environmental management charge' to help fund research and maintenance. Pack your snorkel and flippers, now is the time to dive in and help save the reef!

RELAX, YOU'RE ON ISLAND TIME

Staying on a Whitsunday isle is one of the best options for experiencing the reef. There are 74 islands in total but only eight are inhabited – most are accessed via the wild and trashy port town of Airlie Beach. Our tip: just spend one or two nights at Airlie, then quickly make your way to an island. Most resorts are excessively pricey, but good budget options can be found. Hook Island has a rustic backpacker-style resort with cheap meals, and both Hook and Whitsunday Islands have self-sufficient bush camping areas – perfect for kayaking trips.

HOLGER LEUE » LPI

HARDY REEF, NEAR THE WHITSUNDAY ISLANDS, IS A SPECTACULAR SPOT FOR DIVING AND SNORKELLING

DEFINING EXPERIENCE

A day trip to the outer reef for snorkelling and scuba diving is your must-do. The major tour operators have high-speed catamarans that reach the outer reef – about 40 nautical miles from the mainland – in about two hours. You'll dock at pontoons equipped with scuba-diving training facilities and snorkelling gear for a fun day exploring the colourful coral gardens and marine life. If you prefer dry land, take a day trip to see the pure white silica sands at Whitehaven Beach on Whitsunday Island.

FESTIVALS & EVENTS

✪ You don't have to be a skipper or deckhand to enjoy Australia's largest offshore keelboat regatta, Hamilton Island Race Week, held in late August. Take a stroll down 'Eat Street', packed with international food stalls, then sip on cocktails at the island's bars, or rock out at music gigs on the Marina Tavern forecourt. Bring your credit card – this island is pricey.

✪ During the third week in October, Airlie Beach hosts the Whitsunday Reef Festival featuring a comedy gala, 'dive-in' movies at the lagoon, fashion parades and bands.

LIFE-CHANGING EXPERIENCES

✪ Snorkelling with a bale of sea turtles – some more than 50 years old – just metres from the shore of Hook Island. Hover above them as they scrounge for food on the ocean floor then watch them break the surface to take a rapid, deep breath once every half hour or so.

✪ Spotting a reef shark and feeling your heart in your mouth – only to be told they're as timid as a turtle.

WHAT'S HOT...

Overnight sailing adventures on crewed party yachts with food and booze supplied, stopping off at the best snorkelling spots.

WHAT'S NOT...

Stepping on coral when snorkelling. They're living organisms!

HOT TOPIC OF THE DAY

Coral bleaching: whitening of corals due to increased water temperatures or chemical changes, resulting in starvation, stress and often death. The Great Barrier Reef has experienced two major bleaching events in the past 10 years (2002 and 2006). A major bleaching event in 1998 destroyed up to 16% of the world's coral.

RANDOM FACTS

The Great Barrier Reef:
✪ is 2300 km long,

MICHAEL AW » LPI

✪ has 1500 species of fish, about 400 types of coral and more than 4000 species of molluscs,
✪ has six species of sea turtle and 30 species of whales, dolphins and porpoises.

MOST BIZARRE SIGHT

Moray eels. Creepy, watersnake-like creatures that lurk around the coral reefs. Typically harmless, but a real eye-opener.

DEFINING DIFFERENCE

Whale watching. See humpback and minke whales migrate in pods around the Whitsundays between July and September.

'The West Coast states…mean wide-open spaces and a fresh look at urban and rural living, which has resulted in a fervent eco-movement.'

By Lucy Burningham

WEST COAST, USA

- ✪ **POPULATION** 47.5 MILLION
- ✪ **MAIN CITIES** LOS ANGELES, SAN FRANCISCO, PORTLAND, SEATTLE
- ✪ **LANGUAGES** ENGLISH, SPANISH
- ✪ **MAJOR INDUSTRIES** AGRICULTURE, OIL, MINING, ELECTRONICS, FILM & TV INDUSTRY/ENTERTAINMENT, TOURISM, TIMBER, FISHING, COMPUTER SOFTWARE
- ✪ **UNIT OF CURRENCY** US DOLLAR (US$)
- ✪ **COST INDEX** CUP OF COFFEE US$1.50, PINT OF PACIFIC NORTHWEST CRAFT BEER US$4.50, ROOM AT A MIDRANGE HOTEL OR B&B PER NIGHT US$120

RICHARD CUMMINS » LPI

GO GREEN

Postage-stamp-sized states and bleak urban living? Forget about it. The West Coast states of California, Oregon and Washington mean wide-open spaces and a fresh look at urban and rural living, which has resulted in a fervent eco-movement. Don't be surprised to see fleets of government hybrid cars, public bicycle corrals and solar panels on rooftops. Get in on the action by touring urban chicken coops, tasting biodynamic wines or shopping for heirloom vegies at farmers' markets. Then head outdoors. The emphasis on treating the environment with R-E-S-P-E-C-T means decades-old national and public parks, which encompass islands, coastlines, mountain peaks and pristine public beaches, have been well preserved; and they now feature uber-environmentally friendly interpretive centres and campgrounds.

SURF TO SUMMIT

Outdoor lovers have long flocked to these three states for their varied terrain, and while taking a mellow hike or nature walk are two ways to appreciate the outdoors, consider getting your adrenaline fix along the way. In 2011, it's even easier to hang 10 in the surf off sandy SoCal beaches or make a daring early morning summit of Washington's imposing Mt Rainier thanks to burgeoning guiding and gear-rental businesses. Poach powder on the ski slopes surrounding Lake Tahoe, raft the whitewater on the Rogue River, or strap yourself into a kiteboard harness and rip through the choppy waters of the Columbia River. Still itchin' for a thrill? Hop on a mountain bike and swoop through any number of the thousands of miles of singletrack that snake through the region.

DEFINING EXPERIENCE

After walking across the span of the iconic Golden Gate Bridge, cruise across the bay by ferry to Alcatraz Island, a former federal prison famous for its escape attempts. End the day at the Chez Panisse restaurant in Berkeley, one of

ANGUS OBORN » LPI

the original inspirations for the 'locavore' movement, and dine on some fresh, locally sourced fare, from nettles to truffles.

FESTIVALS & EVENTS

✪ San Francisco's version of the Gay Pride celebration, held for two days every June, culminates in a huge parade that includes Dykes on Bikes, kinky leather-clad crews and plenty of rainbow flags.

✪ In July, beer geeks from around the world gather in Portland for the Oregon Brewers Festival, which features a huge, raucous outdoor beer garden along the Willamette River.

✪ Bumbershoot, held during September each year, has become Seattle's biggest arts and music festival, with tons of live music, dance, theatre, readings and visual arts displays.

LIFE-CHANGING EXPERIENCES

✪ Careening down Mr Toad's Wild Ride mountain-bike trail in South Lake Tahoe.

✪ Standing on the lip of Mt St Helens and imagining the eruption that blew the top off the mountain in 1980.

✪ Diving into the bracing, clear blue waters of Crater Lake, the deepest lake in the US.

WHAT'S HOT...

Cow sharing with friends. Classic cocktails. Dutch bicycles.

WHAT'S NOT...

Car chases. The paparazzi. California's budget crisis.

RANDOM FACTS

✪ Powell's Books, the largest independent bookstore in the world, has 1 million volumes in its downtown Portland location.

✪ One in four Californians was born outside of the US.

MOST BIZARRE SIGHT

The world's largest thermometer, towering more than 40m above the ground in Baker, California, digitally records the sweltering desert heat of the Mojave Desert – a reality check if you're cruising through the valley with the air-con cranked up.

REGIONAL FLAVOURS

Westerners enjoy the melting pot of flavours from the varied immigrant population; there's nothing strange about eating Vietnamese for lunch then Mexican mole for dinner. Meals happen outdoors as much as possible. Even during inclement weather, you'll find Westerners under covered patios wearing jackets, sipping locally made craft beers and noshing on seasonal foods.

'This is the great outdoors – complete with wildly fluctuating weather, massive glaciers, active volcanoes, and herds of graceful guanaco…'

○ CHILEAN PATAGONIA

By Bridget Gleeson

CHILEAN PATAGONIA

- ✪ **POPULATION**: 210,000
- ✪ **PERSON TO SQ-KM RATIO IN AISÉN PROVINCE** ONE TO ONE
- ✪ **MAIN TOWNS** PUNTA ARENAS, COYHAIQUE, PUERTO WILLIAMS
- ✪ **LANGUAGES** SPANISH
- ✪ **MAJOR INDUSTRIES** MINING, SHEEP FARMING, TOURISM
- ✪ **UNIT OF CURRENCY** CHILEAN PESO (CH$)
- ✪ **COST INDEX** *PISCO SOUR* (GRAPE-BRANDY COCKTAIL) CH$1500 (US$2.90), DOUBLE ROOM IN MIDRANGE GUESTHOUSE CH$35,000 (US$68)

THE END OF THE WORLD AS WE KNOW IT

With frozen fingers, you clutch the trail map. A gust of icy wind nearly blows you off the path as a sudden snowstorm rapidly obscures the famed mountain peaks you've come so far to see. Later, after warming up by the fire, you return to your campsite only to realise that your tent is gone with the wind – it'll just be you and your zero-degree sleeping bag tonight.

The dramatic landscape of Chilean Patagonia is not for the faint of heart. But on a crowded planet, it's strangely satisfying to encounter wide open spaces where GPS devices may not help you find your destination and your Gore-Tex jacket does little to protect you from the elements. This is the great outdoors – complete with wildly fluctuating weather, massive glaciers, active volcanoes, and herds of graceful guanaco hightailing it across jaw-dropping mountain vistas.

GRANT DIXON » LPI

GET THAT COOL HOLIDAY SNAP IN PATAGONIA, PERHAPS AT THIS ICE CAVE IN THE MARCONI GLACIER

KAYAKS & CRUISE SHIPS

The region's legendary national parks have long drawn backpackers who dream of paddling to penguin colonies, sailing the Beagle Channel and hiking the 'W' circuit in Parque Nacional Torres del Paine. But as Chile pushes to improve its tourist infrastructure, the region is attracting a higher-end clientele who view the wildlife from the windows of luxury cruise liners.

The recent implementation of a new law designed to professionalise tourism operations throughout the nation signified another thrust forward and serves as a reminder that the desolate mountainscape and clear waters of Patagonia won't always be so untouched.

DEFINING EXPERIENCE

Catch a motorboat into Parque Nacional Bernardo O'Higgins, a national park only accessible by water, and trek to the base of the grand Glaciar Serrano. Toast your fellow hikers with a *pisco sour* (grape-brandy cocktail) shaken with glacier ice, then transfer to a Zodiac raft and cruise through the Southern Ice Field on your way to Torres del Paine.

AMAZING RACE

The Wenger Patagonian Expedition Race is an annual event in which teams of thrill-seeking athletes from all over the world trek, climb, bike and kayak through hundreds of kilometres of Patagonian wilderness. At the time of writing, the 2011 race location had not yet been decided, though the race director hinted that the course will likely involve extensive kayaking in Patagonia's glacier-fed fjords.

ONWARD & FORWARD

Recent natural disasters and unlucky events – from the Infectious Salmon Anemia Virus that left many Patagonian fishermen jobless, to the 8.8-magnitude earthquake that rocked Chile on 27 February 2010 and kept frightened foreigners away for months afterward – have motivated locals to reconsider the value of the tourist dollar. Former salmon farmers on Chiloé Island now lead travellers on excursions to observe giant blue whales, and throughout the nation, hotels and restaurants are eager for your business. So, go ahead, splurge on seafood! (Like you needed an excuse.)

RANDOM FACTS

✪ The last full-blooded member of the Yaghan tribe – the original inhabitants of Tierra del Fuego – still lives on Isla Navarino in Chilean Patagonia. Cristina Calderón is the only person in the world who speaks the tribal language fluently; in 2005, she published a book entitled *Hai Kur Mamashu Shis* (I Want To Tell You A Story).

GARETH MCCORMACK » LPI

✪ The largest concentration of ichthyosaur fossils in the southern hemisphere is located in Torres del Paine. These predatory reptiles, sometimes referred to as 'fish lizards', swam through the region's icy sea 200 million years ago.

✪ The strange case of a 'disappearing lake' – a large body of water in Magallanes that seemed to vanish overnight leaving behind only a deep crater – was widely reported in 2007. Glacier experts blamed ice mechanics and called the event 'not at all unusual'.

REGIONAL FLAVOURS

Thanks to the chilly temperatures and strenuous outdoor activity, you'll work up a roaring appetite in Chilean Patagonia. The cold-weather cuisine, featuring hearty cuts of steak, *cordero* (lamb) and *jabalí* (wild boar) as well as seafood like fresh *trucha* (trout) and *centolla* (king crab), is best savoured – if you can swing it – at a lively *asado* (barbecue) with locals who know how to fire up a grill and keep the meat coming.

'Brilliant snorkelling and diving among sea turtles, sharks and rays can fill days or you can just drift off on a beachside bed.'

NORTH AMERICA

EUROPE

ASIA

AFRICA

SOUTH AMERICA

© GILI ISLANDS

AUSTRALIA

By Ryan Ver Berkmoes

10

GILI ISLANDS, INDONESIA

✪ **POPULATION** 3000

✪ **VISITORS PER YEAR** NO OFFICIAL FIGURES; ESTIMATES VARY WIDELY

✪ **LANGUAGES** INDONESIAN, ENGLISH

✪ **UNIT OF CURRENCY** INDONESIAN RUPIAH (RP)

✪ **MAJOR INDUSTRY** TOURISM

✪ **COST INDEX** ICE-COLD BINTANG ON THE BEACH 15,000RP (US$1.65), SIMPLE BEACHSIDE DOUBLE UNDER 400,000RP (US$44), SNORKELLING BOAT TRIP AROUND THE ISLANDS 100,000RP (US$11)

PETER PTSCHELINZEW » LPI

ISLANDS APART

Swaths of glistening white sand ringing three small palm-fringed islands seemingly afloat amid clear turquoise waters add up to an ideal tropical cliché, and if this was all the Gili Islands had to offer, they'd still get plenty of visitors each year. But what makes these tautologically named isles irresistible ('gili' means 'island' in Indonesian) is a laid-back vibe overlaid with an anything-goes hedonistic energy.

Although the trendy tag 'New Ibiza' is wildly off the mark, the lures here seduce visitors so that days flow into nights and weeks drift past in a haze. Brilliant snorkelling and diving among sea turtles, sharks and rays can fill days or you can just drift off on a beachside bed. There aren't any cars or motorbikes to spoil the mood, rather you can quickly make an island circuit on foot, bike or horse-drawn cart (the latter with little sleigh bells ringing).

Nights are the bomb on Gili Trawangan, by far the most popular of the three islands. All-night parties and raves anchor the weekly calendar (and are in fact the only diary entries) while visitors can choose to sleep it off in original thatched huts a coconut's throw from the beach, in hippy chic retreats where a funky vibe combines with cushy languor, or in stylish villas dripping luxe. Clubbers, scenesters, divers and progeny of the island's original hippy visitors combine in a frothy mix you won't find on neighbouring – and easily seen – Lombok or Bali.

Gili Air might be the ultimate sleep-off destination as it has the mix of comfy, sandy accommodation without the frenetic party pace. Meanwhile the middle of the three,

TIM ROCK » LPI

Gili Meno, sits in high-profile isolation, with a smattering of bamboo bungalows and homestays attracting a fraction of the visitors to nearby Gili T.

DEFINING EXPERIENCE

Awake to the distant put-put of a boat bringing over a new load of Bintang and stumble over to a beachside cafe for a restorative breakfast. Hop on a small boat for a lazy tour of the best snorkelling spots and plunge into the embracing and warm waters in the hope of befriending a sea turtle. Find a shady, sandy idyll for a lost afternoon, then go for a wander looking for new friends, old friends and the perfect twilight cocktail.

FESTIVALS & EVENTS

Week to week, the Gilis have a nearly highlight-free calendar (except for the party nights Gili T bars have staked out for themselves), with one day flowing seamlessly into the next. On a month-to-month basis, the relaxed piety of the mostly Islamic locals adds some welcome texture, although dates vary from year to year on the Western calendar:
✪ Ramadan (1–30 August 2011) – while Gili residents spend the month fasting, the biggest change noted by visitors will be a suspension of all-night parties on Gili T.
✪ Mandi Safar (around 2 February 2011) – at the end of the second month of the Islamic calendar, the often surprisingly waterphobic locals venture down to the beach for a ritual cleansing ceremony that includes a dip in the sea, drumming, readings and a release into the waves of mango leaves bearing prayers.

RANDOM FACTS

✪ Serene Gili Meno is a suitable spot for a hatchery that releases up to 300 sea turtles into the surrounding waters annually.
✪ After years of visitors arriving like mafia mules with pockets bulging with cash, Gili T now has ATMs.
✪ More and more visitors are going direct to the Gilis from Bali on any of several fast daily boats (a little over two hours, about US$65 one way), skipping the un-mellow hassles of Lombok ports.

DEFINING DIFFERENCE

The Gilis are oddballs in almost every sense, from the free spirits who flock here to the very residents themselves. Long uninhabited, the Gilis became home to a wandering band of ethnic Bugis people from Sulawesi just a few decades ago. Initially they fished the rich waters but after a few early hippy travellers washed ashore, the Bugis became adept at reeling in a more lucrative catch. And unlike Bali and Lombok, which are volcanic in origin, the Gilis are formed from coral, making them real anomalies (and giving them the whitest sand in the region).

094
NEW YORK CITY

098
TANGIER

102
TEL AVIV

106
WELLINGTON

110
VALENCIA

LONELY PLANET'S
TOP 10 CITIES

114
IQUITOS

118
GHENT

122
DELHI

126
NEWCASTLE

130
CHIANG MAI

'For all of New York, 11 September 2011 will be a defining moment.'

By Robert Reid

01

NEW YORK CITY

- ✪ **POPULATION** 8.4 MILLION (METROPOLITAN AREA 19 MILLION)
- ✪ **FOREIGN VISITORS PER YEAR** 7.5 MILLION
- ✪ **LANGUAGE** ENGLISH
- ✪ **UNIT OF CURRENCY** US DOLLAR (US$)
- ✪ **COST INDEX** CUP OF COFFEE US$2, HOTEL DOUBLE/DORM FROM US$175/40, SHORT TAXI RIDE US$6, INTERNET ACCESS PER HOUR US$1

COREY WISE » LPI

A BIG YEAR

Since 9/11, the site of the World Trade Center's twin towers has stood out as a closed-off, out-of-view, painful gaping void. This year that changes, as the former WTC site finally reopens to the public with the National September 11 Memorial, a 6-acre, tree-filled plaza with 30ft-deep waterfalls at the footprint of the former towers, rimmed by the name of each victim and illuminated at night (its museum will follow in 2012). For the city, this will be more momentous than if the Yankees, Knicks, Rangers and Giants won simultaneous championships while the ball dropped in Times Square on New Year's Eve. For all of New York, 11 September 2011 will be a defining moment.

COREY WISE » LPI

NEW NEW YORK

Though pockets of history live on, it's in New York's DNA to raze, rebuild, redefine (for example, bulldozing Pennsylvania Station in 1963 to build butt-ugly Madison Square Garden). In recent years, New York's been taking some steps to give back. Half of Times Square's roads were given over to pedestrians, and the 85-acre Brooklyn Bridge Park continues to transform old piers into parks and (more controversially) apartments. Running through Chelsea, the universally loved High Line, a reinvention of an elevated train line as a landscaped walkway, opens its second stretch this year. Also coming up, Brooklyn's Coney Island finishes its much needed $30 million makeover before summer.

DEFINING EXPERIENCE

A first-timer will be awestruck by sights rendered familiar from movies and TV: walk from Central Park to Times Square, then to the Empire State Building, or ride the subway to Manhattan's southern tip for a (free) trip on the Staten Island Ferry past the Statue of Liberty. Repeat visitors stay enthralled with simple do-it-yourself explorations, like wandering around downtown 'hoods such as SoHo or the East Village, or venturing into buzzing Brooklyn, with the bar/music/art scene of

Williamsburg, underrated Prospect Park, and (possibly) the best slice of pizza in the city. Defining New York? It's a moving target.

FESTIVALS & EVENTS

☢ On 23 May, the New York Public Library turns 100. It will exhibit much of its marvellous collection, which includes one of Thomas Jefferson's copies of the Declaration of Independence.

☢ In September Brooklyn's wonderful Atlantic Antic draws more people every year for its avenue-filling fest of all sorts of food and music (blues, traditional Greek, garage rock, R&B and big bands in pastel suits).

☢ A rare outdoor treat in fall, November's New York City Marathon is a cavalcade of joy, with 40,000-plus runners cheered on by thousands of spectators in all five boroughs.

RANDOM FACTS

☢ Two presidents were inaugurated in New York City. George Washington, and – after the assassination of James Garfield in 1881 – Chester Arthur, whose former home is now an Indian spice shop, where you can eat a *mujaddara* (lentil) sandwich in his former bedroom.

☢ The biggest battle of the American Revolutionary War wasn't its finale at Yorktown, but the lesser-known Battle of Brooklyn, a big British victory in August 1776.

☢ Manhattan is not only bottle-shaped, but its name is a Lenape word sometimes translated as 'place of inebriation.' Got that right.

BEST SHOPPING

To come to New York and not shop? That's practically missing the point. All tastes and budgets are covered. Those needing $3 T-shirts can troll Chinatown's alley souvenir shops or get obscene varieties on St Marks Place in the once-edgier East Village. Meanwhile, *Sex and the City* wannabes look out for (often bruising) 'sample sales' – check DailyCandy's Swirl site (www.swirl.com). See local designers' latest offerings in NoLiTa (North of Little Italy), or pretend it's just a day-in-the-park stroll between the Upper East Side's snobby boutiques on Madison Ave or Midtown's high-end department stores along Fifth Avenue.

CLASSIC PLACE TO STAY

With money to burn, the place to stay is Robert De Niro's fantastic Greenwich Hotel, a stately red-brick building on its namesake street. It not only gives you floor-to-ceiling French doors opening from your room to a flower-filled garden, but a Tribeca address too. This compact neighbourhood just outside Lower Manhattan – 'edgy' for the well-to-do – has a rising dining and drinking scene for all of New York. It's home to a flurry of hot eateries, including De Niro's own Locanda Verde.

'A stylish new Tangier is being created with a dynamic arts community, renovated buildings, great shopping and chic new restaurants.'

NORTH
AMERICA

⊙ TANGIER

ASIA

AFRICA

SOUTH
AMERICA

AUSTRALIA

By Helen Ranger

02

TANGIER, MOROCCO

- ⊙ **POPULATION** 670,000
- ⊙ **FOREIGN VISITORS PER YEAR** 25,000
- ⊙ **LANGUAGES** MOROCCAN ARABIC, FRENCH, SPANISH
- ⊙ **UNIT OF CURRENCY** MOROCCAN DIRHAM (DH)
- ⊙ **COST INDEX** MINT TEA ON THE GRAND SOCCO DH7 (US$0.85), DOUBLE ROOM AT EL-MINZAH HOTEL/HOTEL CONTINENTAL DH2100/400 (US$255/49), SHORT TAXI RIDE DH10 (US$1.20), SATURDAY NIGHT TICKET AT THE TANJAZZ FESTIVAL DH200 (US$24)

CHRISTOPHER WOOD » LPI

TANGIER – TAKE TWO

From its extraordinary position perched on the northwesternmost tip of Africa, Tangier looks in two directions: one face towards Spain and Europe, and the other into Africa. The 'white city' announces a culture excitingly different from that of its close cousins across the water. Tangier has always been of strategic relevance – it was even a wedding present from the Portuguese to Charles II of England in the 17th century – but until recently it was considered sleazy, decayed and depraved.

With the recent arrival of a new city governor, the town beach now sparkles, the hustlers are off the streets and even the taxi drivers are polite. A stylish new Tangier is being created with a dynamic arts community, renovated buildings, great shopping and chic new restaurants. One thing that hasn't changed since Matisse was captivated by the city's light is the pleasure of sipping mint tea at a cafe on the medina's Petit Socco as you people-watch: fashionistas alongside Riffian peasants in striped aprons and pompom-festooned straw hats.

SHOP WITH THE LOCALS IN TANGIER'S MEDINA, FOR ANYTHING FROM KAFTANS AND LEATHER TO FRESH PRODUCE

FRANS LEMMENS » LPI

DEFINING EXPERIENCE

Gaze across the sea to Spain while breakfasting Moroccan-style on the terrace of your Kasbah hotel, then meander through the medina streets for excellent shopping. Pause at the Petit Socco to ponder the Beat poets, heiresses and artists who led louche lives here in the '50s, then exit the medina through the market piled high with glistening olives and live chickens. Head for the American Legation Museum where Morocco's 'Mona Lisa' hangs. Take in a French movie at the art deco Cinéma Rif/Cinémathèque de Tanger, pop into the Galerie Ibn Khaldoun for Mohammed Mrabet's paintings, then toast the Caid (governor) with a glass of Moroccan wine in the Moorish El-Minzah Hotel before dinner at a hole-in-the-wall, fresh-off-the-boat fish restaurant.

FESTIVALS & EVENTS

☼ Local filmmakers are celebrated at the National Film Festival of Tangier each January, which showcases homegrown talent in documentaries, short and full-length-feature films.

☼ Catch the Tarab Festival of World Traditional Music in June – a spectacular program of music from countries around the Mediterranean.

☼ TANJAzz, in September, is now a well-established event with an international program of performers over five evenings (and late into the night) at the Palais des Institutions Italiennes, groovy jazz clubs and lounges.

☼ With echoes of musical influence from across the Straits of Gibraltar, the Tanjalatina Festival in November features the sounds of jazz, salsa and tango.

LIFE-CHANGING EXPERIENCES

☼ Browsing the exquisite embroidery or enjoying a good-value meal at the Darna Women's Community House on Place du 9 Avril 1947 helps support this organisation's work to provide a safe haven for women and girls in need.

☼ Getting smothered in brown goo and then scrubbed fearsomely with a rough glove is all part of the steamy hammam experience that will leave you glowing all over. Try a smart spa in the Ville Nouvelle (New City) or hang out with the locals in a medina hammam.

SOME HISTORY

☼ Morocco was the first country to recognise the newly hatched United States of America in December 1777. George Washington's letter of thanks to the Sultan Moulay Suleyman graces the walls of the elegant American Legation Museum, the only US Historic Landmark on foreign soil.

☼ The heady days of the International Zone after WWII attracted all sorts of expat artists, socialites, eccentrics and spies. Writer Paul Bowles completed his classic *The Sheltering Sky* here; William Burroughs wrote *Naked Lunch*; and Truman Capote was a frequent visitor, along with Brion Gysin, Jack Kerouac and Tennessee Williams.

TANGIER'S MEDINA

From the sultan's palace high in the Kasbah down to the Grand Socco, Tangier's medina boasts hundreds of tiny streets bursting with stylish shops and galleries. Here you'll find peacock-coloured kaftans, Morocco's famous leather crafted into voguish handbags and decor outlets that will have you drooling. The jewel in the turban is Boutique Majid, three treasure-filled floors of Berber jewellery and fabrics, a thousand magic carpets, and clothing, antiques and furniture.

'…scratch underneath the surface and Tel Aviv, or TLV, reveals itself as a truly diverse 21st-century Mediterranean hub.'

By Dan Savery Raz

TEL AVIV, ISRAEL

- ✪ **POPULATION** 393,000
- ✪ **FOREIGN VISITORS PER YEAR** 710,000
- ✪ **LANGUAGES** HEBREW, ENGLISH, ARABIC, HEBRISH
- ✪ **UNIT OF CURRENCY** NEW ISRAELI SHEKEL (NIS)
- ✪ **COST INDEX** CAPPUCCINO 11NIS (US$3), HOSTEL DORM BED/HOTEL DOUBLE FOR A NIGHT 180/330NIS (US$49/90), SHORT TAXI RIDE 25NIS (US$6.80), RESTAURANT MAIN COURSE 50NIS (US$13.60), FALAFEL 16NIS (US$4.35), NIGHTCLUB ENTRY 60NIS (US$16.30)

VIVA TEL AVIV!

Tel Aviv is the total flipside of Jerusalem, a modern Sin City on the sea rather than an ancient Holy City on a hill. Hedonism is the one religion that unites its inhabitants. There are more bars than synagogues, God is a DJ and everyone's body is a temple. Yet, scratch underneath the surface and Tel Aviv, or TLV, reveals itself as a truly diverse 21st-century Mediterranean hub. By far the most international city in Israel, Tel Aviv is also home to a large gay community, a kind of San Francisco in the Middle East. Thanks to its university and museums, it is also the greenhouse for Israel's growing art, film and music scenes. In recent years, TLV has been on the tour maps of the world's biggest stars, from Paul McCartney to Madonna and Leonard Cohen. After recovering from an almighty hangover following its 100th birthday celebrations in 2009, Tel Aviv is now looking forward to its second century of progress.

AMANTINI STEFANO » 4CORNERS

FEEL THE RHYTHM OF THE CITY AT TEL AVIV'S DRUMMING BEACH

BAUHAUS TO BOUTIQUE

Like JRR Tolkien's fictional Minas Tirith, Tel Aviv is often called the 'White City'. This nickname refers to its Bauhaus architecture, which received Unesco World Heritage status in 2003. Although nearby Jaffa has been around for some 4000 years, Tel Aviv is still in its infancy. The city only really started to grow in the 1930s with the arrival of modernist German-Jewish architects who fled the Nazis. Nowadays some of these old Bauhaus blocks are looking pretty shabby and so TLV is getting some much needed TLC. Tel Aviv's first town, Neve Tzedek, has been transformed into a tourist and cultural centre lined with boutique shops, galleries and hotels. Somehow the city managed to avoid the worst of the credit crisis and is experiencing a property boom. As the mayor plans to expand the city's business zones, there is no better time to see a city in flux.

DEFINING EXPERIENCE

Bargain your way through the chaotic Carmel Market for a raw slice of the city's past, check out the Tel Aviv Art Museum, then play a game of *matkot* (bat and ball) on Hilton Beach. Next, try eating some of the world's best hummus in the Yemenite Quarter, sipping wine in Neve Tzedek and taking in a dance performance at the Suzanne Dellal Centre. The next day learn how to windsurf on the Med, visit the Diaspora Museum, stroll through Park HaYarkon and cool down with an ice cream on the city's port. Finally, visit the pubs on Nahalat Binyamin St and catch some laser beams at The Block nightclub.

FESTIVALS & EVENTS

✪ The fashionable neighbourhood of Florentine is the place to be on 20 March as thousands of people in fancy dress spill out onto the streets to celebrate the Jewish festival of Purim.
✪ Check out some all-night music on Rothschild Blvd in May, where concert pianists, saxophonists, traditional *klezmer* and funk bands mix it up for Laila Lavan (the White Night).
✪ In June the city comes alive with rainbow flags as it holds the 13th annual Gay Pride Parade, by far the biggest of its kind in the Middle East. The parade of sparkling floats, disco divas and muscle men ends with a huge dance party on the beach.
✪ Part of a triangle that links Tel Aviv, Athens and Istanbul, ArtTLV is an ultracool biennial art event in September that explores multicultural identities.

WHAT'S HOT...

Frozen yoghurt, Facebook, bacon, good hummus, designer shades, gourmet burgers, dogs, rooftop bars, beach volleyball, the '90s.

WHAT'S NOT...

Kosher ice cream, Ahmadinejad, bad hummus, men in thongs, fast food, cats, basement bars, cricket, the '80s.

SARA-JANE CLELAND » LPI

TRIBAL VIBES

There is no better way to start the weekend than dancing along to a hypnotic tribal beat at the Drumming Beach. Every Friday at sundown the Dolphinarium Beach near Jaffa reverberates with this rhythmic gathering of Africans, Israelis and tourists.

BEST SHOPPING

Sometimes called the 'Bubble', Sheinken St is a world away from the air-conditioned malls found elsewhere in the city. Set in the heart of the gay village, it is lined with trendy fashion shops, fruit-shake stalls and the city's best people-watching cafes.

CLASSIC PLACE TO STAY

Housed inside a restored Italian-style villa originally constructed in 1922, the boutique Hotel Montefiore is Tel Aviv's most lavish residence. The restaurant, with a menu described as 'brasserie cuisine under a Vietnamese spell', is fast becoming one of the top places to dine in town.

'…Wellington is Cool-with-a-capital-C, crammed with more bars, cafes and restaurants per capita than New York…'

By Catherine Le Nevez

04

WELLINGTON, NEW ZEALAND

- ✪ **POPULATION** 478,600
- ✪ **FOREIGN VISITORS PER YEAR** 558,000
- ✪ **LANGUAGES** ENGLISH, MAORI
- ✪ **UNIT OF CURRENCY** NEW ZEALAND DOLLAR (NZ$)
- ✪ **COST INDEX** COFFEE NZ$3–4 (US$2.15–2.85), HANDLE (AROUND 430ML) OF BEER NZ$7–9 (US$5–6.40), DOUBLE ROOM AT OHTEL NZ$249–395 (US$177–280), HALF-DAY MOVIE/GOURMET TASTING TOUR NZ$90/$230 (US$64/$164)

OLIVER STREWE » LPI

THE COOLEST LITTLE CAPITAL IN THE WORLD

Kiwi tourism slogans invariably get straight to the point. With its quaint wooden houses tumbling down a ring of hills to the city centre, clustered on reclaimed land around the glittering harbour, in '100% Pure New Zealand', the country's most innovative and inspiring city might just be the 'Best Little Capital in the World'.

Chances are, the slogan writers would have gone for 'Coolest Little Capital in the World', were it not for the unfortunate allusion to the chilly southerlies that gust through the streets.

But despite (or maybe because of) its impetuous weather, Wellington is Cool-with-a-capital-C, crammed with more bars, cafes and restaurants per capita than New York, and a slew of gourmet producers including some 10 independent coffee roasteries. (Wellingtonians are modest-as; they just figure if you're going to do something, why not do it well?) Year-round you'll find arts and cultural events in abundance. Likewise, its film industry, 'Wellywood', centred on the Miramar Peninsula, is booming thanks in large part to the success of Wellingtonian Sir Peter Jackson (executive producer of the 2011 and 2012 *Hobbit* movies currently being made here).

And, even considering the country's population of just under 4.5 million, Wellington is little. Although its the country's second-largest city, it has scarcely one-third the population of Auckland. But its compact size energises its sense of community. Locals *love* their city – jokingly likening it to a cult – and get a kick out of helping visitors fall in love with it too.

Wellingtonians also love their sport, which hereabouts means rugby. This little capital will be front-and-centre on the world stage in 2011 when New Zealand hosts the Rugby World Cup.

PAUL KENNEDY » LPI

DEFINING EXPERIENCE

Take a high-tech voyage through the country's Maori and European history at the national museum, Te Papa; a tour of New Zealand's seat of government and national institutions in the Parliamentary District; or a guided gourmet walk to whet your appetite for Wellington's wealth of eateries. Then peek behind Wellywood's scenes and find your favourite party spot around Courtenay Pl.

FESTIVALS & EVENTS

✪ Wellington's iconic iron sports stadium (nicknamed the 'cake tin') hots up during the electrifying NZI Sevens rugby tournament every February.

✪ Wellington on a Plate dishes up tastings, talks and top restaurant discounts in August.

✪ Out-there clothing and abstract art intersect at September's World of WearableArt (WOW) fashion shows.

✪ Five 2011 Rugby World Cup pool matches (on 11, 17 and 23 September, and 1 and 2 October) and two quarter-finals (8 and 9 October) will take place in Wellington, as well as live-casts and celebrations city-wide.

LIFE-CHANGING EXPERIENCES

✪ Catching the cable car to Wellington's panoramic Botanic Gardens, and stopping to smell its 300 varieties of roses.

✪ Spotting free-roaming kiwi (the birds, not the people) at the 225-hectare, predator-proof oasis, Zealandia.

✪ Blading along Oriental Pde and the bays winding east of the city.

✪ Taking a ferry ride to revegetating Matiu-Somes Island in the centre of Wellington's harbour.

✪ Hiking 4km from the city centre to the volcanic Red Rocks seal colony.

✪ Being mesmerised by the view from Mt Victoria or better still, Brooklyn Hill, beneath its whirring wind turbine.

✪ Meeting local artisans at Sunday's food and wine City Market at Chaffers Dock.

RANDOM FACTS

✪ Wellington is the nation's third capital – following Kororareka (now Russell), until 1840, and Auckland, until 1865 – and the world's most southern.

✪ Filled with everything from vintage vinyl to superstylish restaurants, funky Cuba St was named for an emigrant ship, rather than the island for which the ship was christened. Nevertheless, Cuban namesakes include the iconic cafes Fidel's and Ernesto, both serving locally roasted Havana coffee.

✪ So the stories go, the designer of Wellington's conical parliament building, the Beehive, sketched it as a joke and never intended it to be built.

✪ Some 23% of Wellingtonians are university-qualified, compared with the 8% national average.

MOST BIZARRE LITTLE BAR

Down a blind alley, past the flashing white jumping-rabbit sign and behind a heavy burgundy velvet curtain, the tiny, trippy bar Alice is adorned with distorting mirrors and serves cocktails in china teapots. Following an internal passageway takes you into the adjoining mirror-ball-filled disco extravaganza, Boogie Wonderland.

HIPPEST LITTLE HOTEL

Opened in 2008, the architecturally designed Ohtel has just 10 nouveau-retro rooms furnished with late '50s, '60s and early '70s treasures. Four open on to decks facing Wellington's waterfront.

'…the soaring structures of the City of Arts and Sciences, designed in the main by Santiago Calatrava, Valencia's own son, speak of a new era of splendour.'

By Miles Roddis

05

VALENCIA, SPAIN

- ✪ **POPULATION** 815,400
- ✪ **FOREIGN VISITORS PER YEAR** 1,820,000
- ✪ **LANGUAGES** SPANISH, VALENCIANO
- ✪ **UNIT OF CURRENCY** EURO (€)
- ✪ **COST INDEX** 1L OF PETROL €1.20 (US$1.65), SHORT TAXI RIDE €4.50 (US$6.15), JUG OF *AGUA DE VALENCIA* €18 (US$24.60), GLASS OF *HORCHATA* AND THREE *FARTONS* (LONG FINGER-SHAPED BUNS) €4.60 (US$6.30)

COMING OF AGE

Valencia sits coquettishly and again confidently along Spain's Mediterranean coast. For centuries, it was overshadowed by larger Spanish cities – hardnosed, commercially minded Barcelona and Madrid, the nation's capital. Not any more. While retaining its provincial charm, Spain's third city now mixes with the international crowd. Host of a couple of America's Cup yachting jamborees and an annual street circuit Formula 1 motor race, it's also European Capital of Sport for 2011 and a favourite destination for conferences and congresses.

STRICTLY MODERN & VENERABLY ANCIENT

Valencia enjoyed its golden age two full centuries before the rest of Spain. The sweeping lines of La Lonja, a Unesco World Heritage Site and once the meeting place of the merchant classes, recall the 15th century, when Valencia ruled all the Mediterranean. Half a millennium later, the soaring structures of the City of Arts and Sciences, designed in the main by Santiago Calatrava, Valencia's own son, speak of a new era of splendour.

THE SCULPTURES OF LAS FALLAS SKEWER ALL MANNER OF PUBLIC FIGURES IN THEIR SATIRISING OF CURRENT EVENTS

GREG ELMS » LPI

LAS FALLAS

For nearly a week in mid-March, this springtime bacchanal, Europe's longest and largest street party, is an anarchic, around-the-clock swirl of gunpowder, fire, music and significant overindulgence.

DEFINING EXPERIENCE

Spend the morning at the City of Arts and Sciences, communing with sharks and penguins at the Oceanogràfic, Europe's largest aquarium. Enjoy a beachside paella, here where the dish was first created, at nearby Las Arenas. Walk it off along a stretch of the landscaped former riverbed, a glorious 9km green ribbon that snakes through town. You're heading for Bioparc, an ecofriendly animal park and Valencia's latest major attraction. As dusk falls, sink onto a cafe terrace and enjoy a jug of *Agua de Valencia*, a high-octane concoction of juice from local oranges, *cava* (Spain's Champagne-method bubbly) and whatever spirits take the barman's fancy.

FESTIVALS & EVENTS

In addition to pan-Spain festivals, Valencia celebrates:
✪ Valencia Escena Oberta – two sparkling weeks of alternative theatre and dance in February.
✪ Las Fallas – *fallas* (giant satirical sculptures) fill the streets and draw in some 2 million visitors (15–19 March).

• Feria de Julio – brass bands thumping, bulls running and fireworks galore, climaxing in a magnificent 'battle of the flowers' (late July).
• Día de la Comunidad – processions and elaborate Moros y Cristianos (Moors and Christians) parades celebrate the city's 1238 liberation from Arab occupation (9 October).

LIFE-CHANGING EXPERIENCES

• Enjoying a seagull's panorama over the old town and away to the sea from the top of the cathedral's Miguelete bell tower.
• Dipping *fartons* (long finger-shaped buns) into a cooling glass of *horchata*, Valencia's cloudy, sweet drink made from pressed *chufas* (tiger nuts).
• Lazing on a boat that glides over the Albufera lake at sunset.
• Staying out late to gasp at the Nit de Foc, the most spectacular firework display you'll ever experience.
• Shuddering at the crumps and thuds of *mascletà*, six minutes of heavy artillery explosions at 2pm in the days building up to Las Fallas.
• Wandering among the designer bars, immigrant shops and cool restaurants in the up-and-coming barrio of Russafa.

GREEN HIDEAWAYS

Seek silence among the venerable trees and cacti of the Jardín Botánico, Spain's oldest botanical gardens. Or retreat to the smaller Jardines de Monforte – neat, classical and Valencia's favourite spot for bridal photos.

RANDOM FACTS

• In 2010, with the global recession already biting hard, Valencianos spent €7.44 million on the construction of more than 350 *fallas*, all of which went up in smoke on the fiesta's last night.
• The world's largest paella was created in Valencia; simmering over a giant log fire it measured 20m in diameter and was wolfed down by more than 100,000 people.

MOST BIZARRE SIGHT

Around 100 tonnes of squishy tomatoes flying through the air in La Tomatina, Spain's messiest fiesta, in the outlying town of Buñol.

CLASSIC RESTAURANT EXPERIENCE

Vertical, a relative newcomer, was awarded one Michelin star in almost record time. On the tiptop floor of one of several skyscrapers that have sprung up around the City of Arts and Sciences, it offers heart-stopping views of the complex and, to the east, the sea and port. Its single gourmet menu of small, exquisite dishes changes daily and is described to you at your table.

'Clubs bounce to salsa and rock until the early hours with the vigour you'd expect of Peru's jungle capital, but Iquitos is also a cultural hub…'

NORTH AMERICA

EUROPE

ASIA

AFRICA

○ IQUITOS

SOUTH AMERICA

AUSTRALIA

By Luke Waterson

06

IQUITOS, PERU

- ✪ **POPULATION** 430,000
- ✪ **FOREIGN VISITORS PER YEAR** 50,000
- ✪ **LANGUAGE** SPANISH
- ✪ **UNIT OF CURRENCY** NUEVO SOL (S)
- ✪ **COST INDEX** GLASS OF BEER S5 (US$1.75), HOTEL DOUBLE/DORM BED PER NIGHT S40–100/15–30 (US$14.10–35.30/5.30–10.60), SHORT TAXI RIDE S3–5 (US$1.06–1.75), THREE-DAY JUNGLE TOUR PER PERSON S600–1200 (US$212–423)

SHANNON NACE » LPI

JUNGLE GIANT

After days forging by boat along rainforest-fringed rivers, Iquitos, mighty megalopolis
of the Peruvian Amazon, comes as a shock to the system. Pulsating with life, the city's
latest boom is tourism: visitors may flock to reconnoitre the rainforest but taking time
to imbibe Iquitos itself is imperative too. This is a sultry slice of Amazon life: Brazilian,
Colombian, indigenous and expat. Clubs bounce to salsa and rock until the early hours
with the vigour you'd expect of Peru's jungle capital, but Iquitos is also a cultural hub:
expect works by Peru's top artists, opulent rubber-boom mansions and a museum
on Amazon ethnography for starters. As a trading post for rainforest tribes, market
mayhem and riverboat bustle are part of the package, all conspiring to fill the city with
an addictive, round-the-clock energy.

RAINFOREST FLASH

No, we don't mean sun slanting through the rainforest canopy or sudden exposure to a spider monkey, although there are opportunities for both around town. We're talking oodles of city suavity here, centre of which is the riverfront Malécon – the place to see and be seen, with elegant eateries and bars brimming with beautiful people. It's one of the few spots in the Amazon where you might feel just a little underdressed. Dispense with the jungle clichés: ramshackle huts play second fiddle to hip hostels and hotels, cruise ships ply the water alongside tribal canoes, and rainforest plants are more apparent as flavourings in the local speciality: aphrodisiacal cocktails.

DEFINING EXPERIENCE

The heat makes Iquitos rise at dawn: follow suit, heading to Belén market to browse the myriad stalls stacked with jungle produce. Tribespeople arrive early to tout wares including rare rainforest herbs, marketed as medicine throughout the Western world. On the Malécon, cool bar-cafe La Noche makes a great breakfast break. Next stop: Pilpintuwasi Butterfly Farm, a conservation centre for butterflies and hosts of Amazon animals you may not spot in the jungle proper. For afternoon cooling off, try the pool at La Casa Fitzcarraldo or Laguna Quistacocha, a lake with bars and pedal-boats. Then play a round at the Amazon's only golf course before winding up with an ice-cold beer at river-facing Arandú bar.

PAUL KENNEDY » LPI

FESTIVALS & EVENTS

✪ The big event is San Juan Feast (24 June), an exaggerated, extended version of those daily Iquitos activities of drinking and dancing. The party, in honour of the patron saint of the Amazon, is a celebration of rainforest life. Gorge on *juanes* (rice and chicken wrapped in jungle leaves) and watch the pot pourri of processions (including the dance round the palm trees) unfold. Festivities spill well into the following day.

✪ The Amazon Raft Race is a marathon three-day paddle on log rafts from Nauta to Iquitos, held each September. Teams from around the world compete.

WHAT'S HOT…

Ayahuasca (hallucinogenic jungle vine brew), eco-adventures, strutting your stuff on the riverfront come sundown.

WHAT'S NOT…

Driving safely, drug barons, Huerequeque (the cook from the film *Fitzcarraldo*).

RANDOM FACTS

✪ Iquitos is the only major city not connected to the outside world by road.
✪ Iquitos produces its own beer, Iquiteña, which has garnered a reputation as one of Peru's best brews.
✪ The city has found strange ways to keep itself afloat over the years, selling shamanic medicine, exporting its animals to zoos and even trading jungle vine for use in insecticide to make ends meet.

CLASSIC RESTAURANT EXPERIENCE

Gran Maloka, a glam throwback to the rubber-boom-era heyday, is still top dog in the eating-out style stakes. Leave the humid hubbub of the streets behind and chow down in an air-conditioned mansion with a high-ceilinged tiled interior, wall-length mirrors and silk tablecloths. Bow-tied waiters serve tasty takes on traditional Amazon cuisine for a clientele of well-to-do locals.

CLASSIC PLACE TO STAY

Taking its name from the film by Werner Herzog about an entrepreneur intent on building an opera house in the jungle, La Casa Fitzcarraldo is quite the city oasis: an innovatively-styled B&B in a walled garden. The film crew, Klaus Kinski et al, used the house as a base while making the movie. Individually designed rooms include the mahogany-furnished Mick Jagger suite: the rock singer left his role in the film to do a Rolling Stones tour. The grounds are replete with a pool, bar and treehouse (with wi-fi!).

'Here hides one of Europe's finest panoramas of water, spires and centuries-old grand houses. And it seems the Belgians forgot to tell anyone.'

By Tom Hall

GHENT, BELGIUM

○ **POPULATION** 240,000

○ **FOREIGN VISITORS PER YEAR** 340,000

○ **LANGUAGE** FLEMISH

○ **UNIT OF CURRENCY** EURO (€)

○ **COST INDEX** CUP OF COFFEE €2 (US$2.70), DOUBLE ROOM IN A THREE-STAR HOTEL FOR THE NIGHT €65–90 (US$88–122), SHORT TAXI RIDE €10 (US$13.60), HALF-DAY BIKE HIRE €7 (US$9.50), 250G OF PRALINES (BELGIAN CHOCOLATES) €10 (US$13.60)

EUROPE'S BEST-KEPT SECRET

Here's a secret within a secret: Ghent might just be the best European city you've never thought of visiting, in a country that continues to be criminally overlooked. Ghent hides away in the middle of Belgium's big three – Brussels, Bruges and Antwerp. Most Belgium-bound visitors rushing between these see nothing more than the stately fortifications of Ghent's St Pieter's Station. Those who do hop off the train and stroll along the Leie River to the historic centre will have their eyes out on stalks. Here hides one of Europe's finest panoramas of water, spires and centuries-old grand houses. And it seems the Belgians forgot to tell anyone.

MEDIEVAL & MODERN

For a city with such ancient roots Ghent is one fashion-forward place. Roughly a quarter of the city's population are students, giving the city a young and energetic buzz. Riverbanks and cafes are noisily packed and the atmosphere extends right into the heart of the old city. But this is no place to simply kick back: Ghent has one of Europe's most dynamic festival scenes, which vies for visitors' attention. This year the entire centre will emerge from a major program of rebuilding designed to show off the huge pedestrianised squares. Get here quick, because it won't be long before the rest of Europe gets in on the secret.

FRANK FELL » PHOTOLIBRARY

IF YOU'RE SHOPPING AROUND FOR AN UNDERRATED EUROPEAN DESTINATION LOOK NO FURTHER THAN GHENT

DEFINING EXPERIENCE

Joining the crowds on a sunny day on Graslei and Korenlei, the gorgeous streets lining the Leie, but not before you've taken in the view of it all from St Michael's Bridge. If you've got a few euros in your pocket grab a riverside table and a beer; if not just find a space on the cobbles and join in the impromptu street party. Someone will buy you an ice cream. In the evening head for the Belga Queen restaurant, which is locavore (local food producer) with a twist: everything's sourced from Belgium or made by a Belgian overseas.

RECENT FAD

Ghent is big on anything green, but this comes with a stylish twist. Yes, there are plenty of organic cafes and solar panels everywhere. But vintage shops are the most visible evidence of the philosophy of reduce, reuse and recycle in action and you'll find these dotted all over town. The forward-thinking tourist information office is producing a tailored vintage shopping itinerary for visitors.

FESTIVALS & EVENTS

✪ Gentse Feesten – street performances, a huge dance party, free concerts and parades mark this marvellous 10-day festival in July.
✪ Festival of Flanders in Ghent (17 September to 9 October 2011) – expect fireworks and classical music galore at this cultural extravaganza.
✪ Six Days of Ghent – a classic track event in cycling-mad Belgium, held in November. It causes a great deal of excitement among the bike-loving burghers of Ghent; expect six nights of thrilling, high-speed races and attendant trackside entertainment.

RANDOM FACTS

Ecofriendly Ghent governors encourage meat-free Thursdays, marvellously called Donderdag Veggiedag. As well as local school and government canteens going heavy on the lentils once a week you can expect to have a street map highlighting vegetarian cafes thrust into your hand. This unusually far-sighted move attempts to focus attention on the environmental impact of the meat industry rather than affection for our furry yet edible friends.

MOST BIZARRE SIGHT

Once you're done losing yourself in St Bavo's Cathedral's *Adoration of the Mystic Lamb*, one of the great achievements of Western art, seek out a more modern kind of self-expression. In a bid to stop the spraycan-happy street artists of Ghent redecorating the historic centre, a long, winding alleyway was designated as a free zone for street art. Werregarenstraatje may be one of the town's harder to pronounce names, but

WAYNE WALTON » LPI

Graffiti Street will be a name on the lips of anyone under 30. You're sure to find at least one urban warrior hard at work.

MOST UNUSUAL PLACE TO STAY

Midway between Ghent and Antwerp is the Verbeke Foundation, an astonishing place that is part incubator of outlandish artistic concepts and part both indoor and outdoor art gallery. You can spend the night here in CasAnus, the creation of Dutch designer Joep van Lieshout. As the name suggests, it is an anatomically correct human digestive system on a giant scale fitted out for sleeping. A night here, one of the world's most unique places to stay, will set you back €120. Entry to the room is, only slightly disappointingly, through a side door.

'The great metropolis of Delhi, encompassing Old and New Delhi and sprawling out for miles, has not looked this smart and sparkling in centuries.'

NORTH AMERICA

ASIA
○ DELHI

AFRICA

SOUTH AMERICA

AUSTRALIA

By Abigail Hole

DELHI, INDIA

○ **POPULATION** 12.6 MILLION

○ **FOREIGN VISITORS PER YEAR** 1.9 MILLION

○ **LANGUAGES** HINDI, ENGLISH

○ **UNIT OF CURRENCY** INDIAN RUPEE (RS)

○ **COST INDEX** CUP OF COFFEE RS25–100 (US$0.57–2.25), HOTEL DOUBLE/ DORM ROOM FOR A NIGHT RS200–10,000/100 (US$4.50–226/2.26), METRO TICKET RS8–30 (US$0.18–0.68), INTERNET ACCESS PER HOUR RS30 (US$0.68), DOMESTIC WORKER'S PAY PER MONTH AROUND RS2000 (US$45), LOUIS VUITTON HANDBAG FROM AROUND RS60,000 (US$1355)

KRZYSZTOF DYDYNSKI » LPI

FRESH AS A DAISY

The great metropolis of Delhi, encompassing Old and New Delhi and sprawling out for miles, has not looked this smart and sparkling in centuries. Huge preparations for the Commonwealth Games, which took place in October 2010, improved the city's infrastructure, cleaned up its streets and added to its accommodation options. Aside from, of course, a bounty of new or improved sporting facilities, there's the marvellous artery of the Metro – an underground transport system that's a futuristic, egalitarian world away from the sometimes chaotic, class-ridden situation above ground.

LATEST INCARNATION

This year marks 100 years since New Delhi was founded in 1911. At least eight cities are known to have been founded on this spot. The first four were to the south around the area of Qutb Minar; the fifth (Firozabad) and sixth (Purana Qila) were in present-day New Delhi; the seventh, Shahjahanabad, roughly corresponded to the area of Old Delhi, and the British constructed the eighth. New Delhi still contains the wide tree-lined avenues and triumphalist colonial architecture that is nevertheless, thoroughly Indian – the area today forms Delhi's political heart. The commemoration of this anniversary is sure to be a colourful and lively affair.

CHRISTER FREDRIKSSON » LPI

DEFINING EXPERIENCE

For a taste of Old Delhi, wander around the broken splendour of the Red Fort and plunge into the tumultuous backstreets to discover the Jama Masjid, India's largest mosque. Next, New Delhi: visit Indira Gandhi Smriti and learn something of the dynasty that has dominated modern Indian politics. Then, await dusk in the Mughal gardens around Humayan's Tomb, hear *qawwali* (devotional songs) at the Hazrat Nizam-ud-din Dargah, then sip a cocktail at the sublimely decadent 1911 bar at the Imperial Hotel.

FESTIVALS & EVENTS

✪ On 26 January, Republic Day, the founding of the independent Republic is remembered in New Delhi, when a flag-hoisting ceremony by India's president is followed by an enormous military parade down Rajpath. The end of the celebrations is marked on 29 January, at the Beating of the Retreat.

⊙ The 2011 ICC Cricket World Cup takes place in February and March, hosted by India, Sri Lanka and Bangladesh, with 14 international cricket teams competing in a series of One Day Internationals. Watch the entire Indian nation go even more cricket-crazy than ever.

⊙ In October, the massive ramparts of Delhi's 16th-century fort Purana Qila make a superb backdrop for the Ananya Festival of classical dance, while the Qutub Festival of devotional music presents world-renowned performers of Indian classical and folk music, singing and dancing in the beautiful setting of Qutb Minar.

WHAT'S HOT...

The economy: despite global conditions, the Indian economy has continued to boom and is projected to grow by 8.5% this year.

WHAT'S NOT...

Autorickshaws – noisy, smelly, ubiquitous, and also the best and quickest way to get around an often gridlocked city. But RIP the Delhi auto, which has been read the last rites as part of clean-up measures.

HOT TOPICS OF THE DAY

Cricket, cricket, cricket. Always a hot topic of conversation, but never more than this year, when most of the World Cup games will take place in India, with several in Delhi itself. When not talking about cricket, you could hotly debate the Women's Reservation Bill, which passed India's upper house of parliament in 2010, setting the stage for women to hold one-third of all legislative seats.

MOST BIZARRE SIGHT

Sulabh International Museum of Toilets dishes the dirt on toilets from 2500 BC to the present day. But this museum is much more than a mere curiosity: Sulabh International has done much essential work in the field of sanitation, helping with the education of children born into a career of 'manual scavenging' (toilet scraping), enabling them to do other work, as well as developing pour flush toilets and bio-gas plants.

CLASSIC PLACE TO STAY

At the British Raj–era Imperial on Janpath in New Delhi, the marble-lined, chandelier-hung hallways purr with opulence, there's a fantastic collection of 17th- and 18th-century paintings throughout, and the high-ceilinged rooms are immaculate, cosy and luxurious. To celebrate 100 years of New Delhi in style, this is the place to stay, but if you can't afford the US$500 for a double, perhaps you can stretch to a cocktail in the bar, which is named 1911, of course.

'Today's 'new' Newcastle is a unique blend of imagination, sophistication and laid-back surf culture.'

NORTH AMERICA

EUROPE

ASIA

AFRICA

SOUTH AMERICA

AUSTRALIA

○ NEWCASTLE

By Catherine Le Nevez

09

NEWCASTLE, AUSTRALIA

- ○ **POPULATION** 532,500
- ○ **FOREIGN VISITORS PER YEAR** 112,300
- ○ **LANGUAGE** ENGLISH
- ○ **UNIT OF CURRENCY** AUSTRALIAN DOLLAR (A$)
- ○ **COST INDEX** DORM BED A$28–32 (US$26–29.80), SCHOONER (425ML) OF BEER A$4.90 (US$4.55), 80-MINUTE GROUP SURF LESSON A$30 (US$28)

AUSTRALIA'S MOST UNDERRATED CITY?

Anyone surprised to see Newcastle on the list of 2011's hottest cities (and there's a few of you, right?) probably hasn't pulled in off the Pacific Highway, or at least not for a while.

Newcastle flies under the radar of Aussies and international travellers in part because it's overshadowed by its bigger, bolder and better-known sibling, Sydney, 150km south. But, at around one-tenth the size, Australia's second-oldest city has Sydney-like assets: surf beaches, a sun-drenched subtropical climate, and diverse dining, nightlife and arts.

Not only is Newcastle ideally located just two hours by road or rail or 30 minutes by plane or seaplane from Sydney, it's less than an hour's drive west to the Hunter Valley wineries, south to sailboat-filled Lake Macquarie, north to whale-watching and shark-feeding at Port Stephens and to sandboarding at Stockton Beach (the southern end of the 32km-long beach is a five-minute ferry ride across Newcastle's harbour).

FROM 'STEEL CITY' TO CREATIVE HUB

In part, too, Newcastle is often bypassed due its long-time reputation as an industrial city. But while it's the world's largest coal-export port, it's won numerous awards for environmental conservation and clean beaches.

For the best part of a century, Newcastle was dominated by its billowing steelworks until their closure in 1999 dealt a massive economic blow. But Novocastrians (Newcastle residents) are a resilient bunch, and the dozen intervening years have seen an explosion of artists taking advantage of the cheap living costs. Newcastle now has the most artists per capita nationwide, and the most galleries – from acclaimed regional centres to independent, artist-run spaces and dozens of disused city-centre buildings occupied by photographers, fashion designers, digital artists and more as part of the inner-city regeneration scheme, Renew Newcastle.

Today's 'new' Newcastle is a unique blend of imagination, sophistication and laid-back surf culture.

EMMA HARM » CORBIS

YOU DON'T NEED A BIRD'S-EYE VIEW TO APPRECIATE SEASIDE LIFE IN NEWCASTLE

DEFINING EXPERIENCE

Brekkie at a beachside cafe, browsing Darby St's off-beat boutiques, deliberating over Beaumont St's 40 eateries, taking a spin in the surrounding regions and settling in at one of the sleek bar/restaurants lining Honeysuckle Wharf on Newcastle's working harbourfront as the afternoon drifts into evening.

FESTIVALS & EVENTS

✪ Year-round, urban public spaces host 100-plus days of mostly free events, from street theatre to installations, concerts, open-air cinema and mass dance classes, as part of the 'L!vesites' program.

✪ Pros battle it out on the peeling right-handers at gazetted surfing reserve Merewether Beach during Surfest in March.

✪ First-time and famous filmmakers produce seven-minute-long films in 24 frenetic hours in July for the world's original Shoot Out Film Festival.

✪ Each October, Newcastle's This Is Not Art Festival breaks traditional and new media ground.

✪ One of several vibrant annual street fairs held throughout the city, November's King Street Fair & Folk Festival features more than 100 market stalls and entertainment including busking comps.

LIFE-CHANGING EXPERIENCES

✪ Paddling out past the breakers at sunrise at one of Newcastle's six surf beaches.

✪ Splashing in the convict-carved Bogey Hole ocean baths below Norfolk Pine–shaded King Edward Park.

✪ Canoeing, cycling or walking through the 45-hectare Hunter Wetlands Centre Australia, home to more than 250 wildlife species.

✪ Cheering on a Newcastle Knights rugby league home game at EnergyAustralia Stadium, to be overhauled by the start of the 2011 season.

✪ Catching up-and-coming local musicians before they hit the big-time at the intimate 1910-built venue, Lizotte's.

RANDOM FACTS

✪ The sand spit Nobbys Head was joined to the mainland in 1846. Local Aboriginal stories tell of a kangaroo that jumped onto the former island and remains within the land, occasionally thumping its tail (hence the sporadic seismic activity). Nobbys' height was halved to 28m in 1855 to keep the wind in ships' sails as they turned into port.

✪ Fort Scratchley was the only Australian fort to return wartime fire at an enemy ship (a Japanese submarine, in 1942).

✪ Sand from Stockton's dunes (the southern hemisphere's largest) is exported to Hawaii.

✪ Famous Novocastrians include all three band members of Silverchair, ex-Newcastle Knights cheerleader and Miss Universe, Jennifer Hawkins, and more Australian Ballet ballerinas than from anywhere else in Australia.

MOST BIZARRE SIGHT

The cheekily nicknamed cylindrical, dome-topped Queens Wharf Tower, thrusting 40m skyward (with a 360-degree city panorama once you've climbed to the top).

CLASSIC CAFE EXPERIENCE

Don't miss Estabar, overlooking Newcastle Beach, for Mediterranean-inspired breakfasts and out-of-this-world hot chocolate; Darby St stalwart Goldbergs, with battered sofas, wax-covered candelabra and a palm-shaded courtyard, for wholesome tofu-burger-type fare; and Scotties, in a bare-boards Newcastle East terrace, for takeaway cones of salt-and-pepper squid and old-fashioned milkshakes through to stylish evening menus.

BEN JEAYES » SHUTTERSTOCK

CARVE IT UP AT ONE OF THE MANY SURF BEACHES IN NEWCASTLE

'With a history dating back further than anyone can remember, its influence remains enormous.'

By Mark Beales

10

CHIANG MAI, THAILAND

- ✪ **POPULATION** 240,000

- ✪ **FOREIGN VISITORS PER YEAR** 1.5 MILLION

- ✪ **LANGUAGE** THAI

- ✪ **UNIT OF CURRENCY** THAI BAHT (B)

- ✪ **NUMBER OF BUDDHIST TEMPLES** 104

- ✪ **COST INDEX** LARGE BOTTLE OF BEER 100B (US$3), HOTEL DOUBLE/DORM BED PER NIGHT 600–2000B/100–150B (US$18–61/3–4.50), BICYCLE RENTAL PER DAY 50B (US$1.50), BOWL OF NOODLES 30B (US$1)

FELIX HUG » LPI

NORTHERN SOUL

If Chiang Mai were a person, it would be Bob Dylan. With a history dating back further than anyone can remember, its influence remains enormous. And despite its great age, there's still a bohemian chic that makes it as relevant and hip as ever. Culture capital of Thailand, Chiang Mai was once the heart of the Lanna kingdom. Today those wanting to flee the bustle of Bangkok visit to lounge in coffee shops and drink in the city's artisanal atmosphere. With a friendly, cosmopolitan feel, this is one easy, safe and pleasant place to explore. There are dozens of well-preserved temples here, too. Many new ecotours and adventure trips are appearing, and with a choice of river rafting, elephant rides, trekking and off-road cycling, even the biggest adrenaline junkie will be sated.

FELIX HUG » LPI

DEFINING EXPERIENCE

Start by sipping an espresso made from homegrown beans at one of the numerous coffee shops. Head inside the old city walls and past the moat to explore Wat Phan Tao, a glorious teak temple, and the neighbouring Wat Chedi Luang, with its elegant black and gold lacquered pillars and partially restored Lanna *chedi* (stupa). Make time to chat to the resident monks in the temple grounds, who are always keen to practise their English. Freshen up with a dip at one of the waterfalls on the way to Wat Phra That Doi Suthep, one of the north's most sacred temples, at the summit of Doi Suthep. Spend the evening milling around the night bazaar, a sprawling, heaving collection of antiques and souvenirs.

FESTIVALS & EVENTS

✪ The handicraft village of Bo Sang, southeast of Chiang Mai, stages an umbrella festival in January. Its streets are filled with an umbrella procession by day and a lantern parade by night.

✪ The three-day Flower Festival in early February includes cultural performances, thousands of blooms and a spectacular parade featuring decorated floats.

✪ King Bhumibol Adulyadej is the world's longest-serving monarch. Major celebrations are planned for Chiang Mai during June 2011 to mark the 65th anniversary of His Majesty's accession to the throne.

⊙ The Chiang Mai Red Cross and Winter Fair, held from late December to early January, is a great opportunity to munch on Thailand's finest northern dishes and watch cultural performances.

LIFE-CHANGING EXPERIENCES
⊙ Swinging through a forest canopy on a zipline as part of the ecofriendly Flight of the Gibbon adventure.
⊙ Trekking and rafting on the way to meeting remote hill-tribe communities, and staying overnight in one of the villages.
⊙ Cycling off-road through picturesque countryside.

RANDOM FACTS
⊙ At 2565m above sea level and just west of Chiang Mai, Doi Inthanon is Thailand's tallest mountain.
⊙ When founded in 1296, the city was considered a living entity. Everything to the north, near the 'head', was sacred, while things in the south, near the 'feet', were less auspicious.
⊙ Lin Ping, the first giant panda born in Thailand, is the star attraction at Chiang Mai Zoo – she even has her own nationwide 24-hour TV show.

MOST BIZARRE SIGHT
With its soothing music, scented oils and courteous staff, the Lila Thai Massage Shop doesn't seem to be that unusual. But all is not as it appears. Every masseuse working here is an inmate at the neighbouring Chiang Mai Women's Prison. This prison initiative to offer the women a chance to learn new skills while inside has been hugely successful, and now the shop does a brisk trade with its genuinely soothing massages.

CLASSIC RESTAURANT EXPERIENCE
Kôw soy, a curried noodle creation, is perhaps Chiang Mai's signature dish. The best place to taste it is at the aptly-named Just Khao Soy restaurant, located on Charoen Prathet Rd. The bowl, full of pickled cabbage, red onions, crispy noodles and a spicy broth, is served on an artist's wooden palette, while diners can add their own condiments.

BEST SHOPPING
The Sunday Walking Street market stretches through the old city with displays of silk, silver and snacks. It's a cross between hip and hippy, with artists sketching portraits, traditional musicians performing on the street and university students selling delicious homemade strawberry wine for 20B (US$0.60) a glass.

136
BEST-VALUE
DESTINATIONS
FOR 2011

140
THE 10 BEST
THINGS TO DO
IN 2011

144
MOST
SUPER-LUXE
TRAVEL

148
TOP 10 PLACES
TO LEARN HOW
TO COOK THE
LOCAL CUISINE

152
BEST PLACES TO
SEE RED

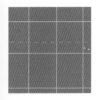

176
BEST
UNDERWATER
EXPERIENCES

180
FIERIEST
FOODS

184
THE GREATEST
COMEBACK
CITIES

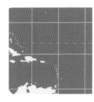

188
10 BEST THINGS
TO CLIMB

192
TOP 10 CITIES
FOR ARTISTIC
INSPIRATION

LONELY PLANET'S
TOP TRAVEL LISTS

156
TOP 10 COUNTRIES THAT DIDN'T EXIST 20 YEARS AGO

160
BEST PLACES FOR DANCE FEVER

164
WORLD'S GREATEST BOOKSHOPS

168
BEST SECRET ISLANDS

172
LAST COLONIES

196
BEST VAMPIRE SPOTTING LOCALES

200
TOP 10 HISTORICAL RE-ENACTMENTS

BEST-VALUE
DESTINATIONS
FOR 2011

THIS BARGAINOUS BOUNTY OF BUDGET-FRIENDLY BOLT-HOLES
WILL HAVE YOUR BANK MANAGER SMILING AND YOU OUT ON THE
ROAD FOR LONGER, FOR LESS.